Golden Boy

Ray Slater Berry

culturatti ink.
A FUNKY LITTLE PUBLISHING HOUSE

Publishing consultant: Erika Parsons

Copyright © 2018 by Ray Slater Berry.

ISBN: 978-0-578-40944-3

Library of Congress Control Number: 2018962654

Printed in the United States of America.

First Printing: 2019

To Falmouth

Acknowledgements

I cannot thank my community enough for helping to make this book happen. Writing can be lonely work, but publishing is not. To my first reader, motivator, and mother for putting up with me. To my father and my sister for keeping me grounded. To Kajsa for her relentless support and to Ivan for his undeniable patience. To Elfrea for telling me I had something worth running with and to Erika for helping me run. Lastly, to Joey, for showing me what love can be and a happiness I hope to one day see again.

17th August

Dear Aiden,

The nurse asked if I was ready to clear out our locker. Her thick, east London accent pulled me from a dreamless slumber. I blinked my way into consciousness as her heavy hands pushed stray hairs from my face and caressed the back of my head. Her full lips pushed into a smile that did not reach her eyes, and I began to focus on the black freckles that dotted her dark skin. I turned my head. The hospital beds around me were taken. Each patient was fast asleep; hopefully their minds were taking them far away from here. Everything was quiet. The silence hung, heavy in the air. I expected such a large, London hospital to be busier, louder, and more alive. The nurse helped me to my feet, and I shuffled out of the ward.

The key was in a little heart-shaped box your aunty Fi gave me. The box once held chocolate truffles, but you kicked for them as soon as I saw them. Still in my floral slippers and matching hospital gown, I walked along the row of school-like lockers in search of ours. The nurse had slicked my hair back into a tight ponytail. I put my hand to the back of my head and felt tufts of hair poking through the band like the leaves of a baby pineapple. The polyester of the gown stuck to my skin, which was now clammy from walking through the hospital corridor. I placed my hand on the bottle-green door of locker number 36 and let the coolness of the brush-painted metal shoot through my skin. I pulled the key from the front pocket of the gown, which sat on my stomach like a kangaroo pouch, and pushed the key into the lock. The lock was awkward. I wobbled the key and lifted the door slightly to pull it open. The creak of the door's hinges echoed through the corridor. I began unloading your gifts. A golden rattle lay alongside a packet of nappies, a bottle of shampoo, and a tub of E45 Cream, all of which had been made into the shape of a wedding cake, each layer a new gift and everything wrapped in cellophane. A white candle was stuck into a tightly rolled blue towel at the top of the tower. The gifts were from your aunty Fi. A pair of knitted woollen socks hung on the door by some blue ribbon. I unhooked them and ran my thumb along the ribbon while I surveyed the rest of the locker. A few tiny T-shirts, some bibs, a onesie, and some bath toys were piled against the back.

"Babe, I'll take that. You go sit down with the little monster." A man's voice brought my attention away from the locker and drew my eyes down the hall to where he was standing in front of one of his own. You could practically hear him smiling through his words.

"Don't be calling him a monster already, Nathan. Kids are what you say they are. That's what my mum used to say."

With woollen socks in hand, I closed the locker door to look at who was talking. A couple that couldn't have been past their mid-twenties was emptying a locker. The woman had taken a seat opposite the locker and was smiling into a bundle of white towels in her arms. Nathan's muscles rippled under his tattooed skin as he worked. Stray pieces of clothing and plastic toys looked small and inadequate alongside his build. He held each item up and frowned at it before throwing it into the bag at his feet. The woman laughed into the bundle, and her cooing voice rang through the otherwise quiet hall. I pulled my door open once more. It was almost empty now save for a stuffed polar bear in the corner. I hadn't noticed him before. I pulled the bear out and wrapped him in the blue towel. I started humming my own tune and brushed the fur from the bear's eyes. The cooing from the woman down the corridor stopped.

"My grandmother used to sing that to me before bed. Where is it from?"

The young woman was looking right at me, a smile on her face, her eyes wide and innocent to the world. Her voice was lighter now that she was no longer addressing Nathan.

I shook my head. "I'm not sure."

"Oh, that's a shame," she said, giving the bundle in her arms a little squeeze.

Nathan, who I presumed to be her partner, laughed. "It's crazy, isn't it...all this crap you get given? We probably aren't going to use half of it. I haven't got a clue what most of it does."

He waggled a onesie at me. It was upside down. The woman just shook her head and smiled. I clutched the polar bear to my chest, running my fingers over the soft fabric. The woman began cooing my song to the bundle in her arms. I went to pick up my now full hospital bag from my feet.

"Let me get that for you. You ladies have done enough for a while." Nathan winked and started towards me.

"No, no honestly it's fine. I've got it," I replied, waving my hands in front of me to ward him off.

"Please," he insisted, just moments from me now.

"I've got it. Thank you."

He was at my side. We both moved to pick up my bag at the same time. The bundle in my arms fell to the floor. He opened his mouth and reached out towards the bundle.

"Fuck!"

The bundle hit the floor, and the polar bear rolled out.

"Language, Nathan!" The woman with the baby scolded from down the hall. Nathan rolled his eyes and smiled back at me.

"For a moment I thought that was your baby," he chuckled, dramatically wiping his brow. I picked up the polar bear.

"Don't be silly, Love. My baby was eight pounds, five ounces; you'd have known if he'd hit the floor."

Nathan's head cocked to one side, he mouthed the sentence I just said.

"I was going to call him Aiden."

The woman's song stopped.

"I'm so sorry."

Nathan began backing up. His frame looked smaller now. He took a few more steps before turning on his heels and heading to his family. I could just make out his jaw moving and his head shaking ever so slightly. I looked past him to see the woman's wide eyes glancing between her partner and me. He reached his partner, pushed an arm under her elbow and helped her to her feet. As the family retreated down the corridor, the woman glanced over her shoulder. I placed the bear and towel into the hospital bag and closed the locker door. I left the key, which smelt of metallic chocolate truffles, in the lock and walked back to our bed.

Dear Aiden,

Returning home with an empty baby carrier was one of the most painful things I have ever had to do. I kept glancing at it in the passenger seat, checking on you, wondering if you'll ever get travelsick. I even strapped the thing in. I actually did it right for the first time in my life. I caught myself speaking to you, reassuring you in that strange, high-pitched voice I've heard so many mothers use and vowed I never would. Your baby blue blanket lined the carrier. I reached across the gear stick to tuck you in and just kept finding lumps of thick air. I pulled over three times to vomit on that 20-minute journey. The third time there was nothing left, and I just retched. I kept trying to cry on the roadside. I kept picturing how women break down in films. I fell to my knees the way I imagined I should. I waited for the rains that always descend on Oscar-winning performers. I pinched my legs and my stomach and dug my nails into my wrists; anything to make the tears come. But the sun continued to shine. The traffic lights ticked from one colour to the next and cars continued to roll by, throwing nothing but fumes into my face. I must have looked like I just had a cramp.

My sister's name is Fiona, but we've been calling her Fi for as long as I can remember. I knew she had been to the house. I could still smell her perfume in the hall. She always smothers herself in it.

I kicked my shoes off and walked through the dimly lit hall to the kitchen. I placed your carrier on the table and surveyed the risk-free space. The corners of the coffee table had a softer, polystyrene edge. Matte white child locks stood out on the glass of the display cabinets. The wooden floor looked bare now that Grandma's rug was in the attic. I walked back into the hall. My tennis rackets were no longer by the front door. Fi must have packed them away. I had them there throughout the entire pregnancy as a visual reminder to stay healthy. They reminded me of the social life I had pre-baby and the life I wanted to cling to well into motherhood. Imagine that, mother turning up to the courts, newborn baby on one arm and tennis rackets packed up in the other. What a sight I would have been!

I headed into the front room. There are so many baby-sized presents piled against one wall and unopened cards addressed to *The Happy Family* and *The Little One*. One day, I'll open them with you. One day, when I'm old and grey and you're still young with that glorious smell babies have, we'll sit on our own little white cloud. We'll open all these cards and presents together. We'll *ooh* and *ahh* over the illustrations. We'll laugh at the jokes, and you'll point at the fancy writing because, one day, you'll be a poet.

What am I supposed to do with a bag that is completely baby ready? The contents from our locker and your baby carrier were sitting on the kitchen table, yet you aren't here to help me use them. I took them upstairs to your nursery and opened the chest of drawers I put together myself. My feet sunk into the plush cream carpet I'd purchased, which was probably a bad idea. I didn't want to look around the room. I wasn't ready to take in what you will never see. I quickly unpacked the contents of our locker and filled your drawers with essentials. I held onto your polar bear for a little longer, imagining your tiny little hands wrapped around his paws. I placed him on top of the chest of drawers so he could look over you.

I placed the baby carrier alongside your chest of drawers and left your room as quietly as I could. I didn't know what to do with myself. I had all these grand ideas of how I was going to give you a tour around the house, saving your room for the very last. Actually, why not? Why can't I still give you the tour? I'm going to put this letter on hold, grab the baby carrier from your room and head downstairs.

"Welcome home, Aiden. Come with me, My Dear, and let me show you around.

Let's start in the hallway, even though it's not the most exciting stop on the tour. The floor is a dark laminate wood, and there's a stained-glass window above the telephone, which sits on a small black coffee table at the bottom of the stairs. On the left side of the table, there's an incredibly large pile of shoes that Mummy probably should have dealt with a long time ago. I'll get to them one day. Above the shoes are all the coats Mummy will never wear. As you head through the hallway the front room is on the right. It looks on to the front garden, which is why I keep the blinds down. We've got a few nosey neighbours that drift by. Mrs. Dewley is probably the worst. You'll meet her one day. She's a sweet lady, and she means well. I guess she's just used to the days when everyone left their front door open, and you could just stroll right on in for a cup of tea. That's not the case anymore, our blinds stay down, and our front door locks automatically as soon as you close it.

The kitchen is where I imagine us spending most of our days; hence the polystyrene covered corners. Looking over the dining area, I can see us piecing giant puzzles together on the table. I can see me testing the temperature of your milk with one hand while bouncing you on my knee. I can see you pulling at cupboard doors and your little hands grabbing anything within reach. Let me slide open the patio door and take you out back. The garden isn't much; it's got a small patio and a patch of grass with a washing line running across the middle of it. It'll be big enough for us, for now.

Let's head back inside. I want to show you the bathroom. I envision you as a water baby. It was one of the first daydreams I had after finding out I was pregnant with you. I pictured your little stocky legs kicking in the pool while I held you horizontally. I pictured holding you above the water while I disappeared underneath before reappearing pulling a different face. I pictured you chuckling, blowing little spit bubbles and snot as you laughed.

Do you want to see your bedroom? Your name is carved into this mahogany plaque I nailed to your bedroom door. The wood is smooth, polished, and it feels cold under my touch as I run my fingers along the outlines of your letters. Okay, Aiden, I'm going to open your door, so you can see what I did with your nursery. I hope you like the shade of blue I painted your walls. I know it's not exactly imaginative, but I didn't want to go overboard with colours. That's your cot in the corner next to the window. And over there, along the left-hand side of the room, is your chest of drawers. That's a dream catcher hanging in the window. It's made of carved, multi-coloured, shaved glass. It catches the sunlight, and throws every colour of the rainbow through your dreams and across your walls. Do you like it, Darling? Welcome home."

Dear Aiden,

I went out earlier today and bought 13 cans of *Daffodil White* paint. I was drawn to it because daffodils provide a promise of new life. I brought the cans up to your room and began to drown out the baby blue walls with it. I have been careless. Paint is everywhere and not in a cute, movie kind of way. Flecks of paint have spat on your cot and drawers. Your room is a mess. I've been too quick to get the job done. Paint is dripping down the skirting board and onto the carpet. I began to get frustrated the more I realised how much I was messing this up. I'm sorry, Love. I just want a clean start for us both. I didn't mean for your room to end up like this. Your favourite teddy—the polar bear—just stares at me with his dull button eyes. I can tell he's questioning my motives and why I am so quick to leave you in the past. His permanent grin is mocking me.

You never even met him, I thought. I threw the paintbrush at the bear's head. *You didn't know him. I knew him.* The brush narrowly missed the bear and dented the plasterwork behind him. I stormed across the room, my vision blurred, and a red haze overcame my sight. I snatched the bear from his resting place: *He was my little boy. My Aiden. Not yours, and not anyone else's. Who had the right to take him away from me? My boy had a heart of gold.*

That's something you'll never have. I tore the bear's mocking head off and broke a nail in the process. I pulled out each and every bit of his stuffing until the walls were covered in little white specks of the bear's fluff. They stuck to the wet paint, yet still no tears came, not for the bear, not for you.

"Barb! Are you home?" I heard Fi's voice downstairs.

I ran to your bedroom door, reached up to the lock—which you wouldn't be able to use until you were way into your teens— and slid the bolt across.

"Barbara? Honey? Everything okay?" Fi asked.

I thought that if I could avoid telling anyone then I could convince myself for a little bit longer that the doctors had worked a miracle and saved my little boy. Maybe they would bring you through my front door with bells and whistles and a television crew behind them. The presenter would jump out and exclaim: "Barbara Bridges, you've been pranked." How we'd all laugh.

"Barbara? Love? Do you want to come out and talk?" Your aunty Fi was talking to me outside your door. I leaned my back against the door and slid down it. I could picture my sister doing the same thing on the other side. I could feel she was there—my mirror image—in another dimension.

The streetlights eventually blinked out, and for a while everything was black. I sat through it all, every star winking in and out for the night. Each one doing the rounds, checking in on our tired town as it slept. I imagined the stars watching over young men, wearing suits by day, and then coming home to sleep like babies in the arms of their wives. I imagined the same stars teaming together with the moon to light the night's path for those who remained there, the drunks, the homeless, and the tearaway teens. I imagined these stars, picking up the wishes of the children from the local primary school, your school, churning them over and seeing what they could create for the night's work.

A few brave rays of the morning began to reflect off the jewels of your dream catcher sending beams of golden light across your now blue and white walls. The familiar sound of my sister's knees cracking sliced through the morning calm. The door behind me bowed a little as she leaned against it to get up. There was a muffled fumbling from the other side of the door and a note slid underneath. The thud, thud, thud of the stairs and the quieter creak of the third to last one at the bottom let me know she had left.

"I'll leave some food in the fridge for you.

Fi. X"

I closed my eyes. The dream catcher sent shades of light across the backs of my eyelids. All I could smell was our new start. Deep breaths, Love. With each breath, I can breathe in more of you. I pictured us in this room. I saw myself dipping a finger in some whiskey and dropping it on your tongue to help send you off to sleep. I imagined humming to you while I rocked you to sleep in my arms before oh-so-carefully lowering you into your cot. I pictured restless nights with you. Your cries would ring loud in my ears, and I would try to figure out what you needed. I would try to read the knots of your fists or the anguish in your stormy eyes.

I daydreamed: *You don't need changing. I fed you an hour ago. What's wrong, Love? How can I make these tears go away?* I would take in every curve of your sweet angelic face while your fingers and toes twitched in dreams I'll never hear about and you'll never remember. I hope those dreams are taking you to a better place now. Deep breaths. I'll join you one day. We'll move in dreams together.

My head was dizzy, and my vision was hazy. I walked over to your chest of drawers, opened one near the top and pulled out your golden rattle. I twirled it in my hands and let the beads tumble around inside. I let it rain. I continued to twirl the rattle as I circled the room. I ran my hands along the walls and let the drying paint and clumps of bear fluff cover my fingers. I raised them to my face and breathed in as much of you as I possibly could.

I felt so close to you, Love. I curled up on the carpet next to your cot. I pulled what was left of your polar bear to my chest, tapped the rattle against the floor, and fell into a sleep filled with dreams that were not mine.

I woke with a start a few hours later, shivering from the cold. I didn't realise it could get so cold in your room. I'll have to remember that for tomorrow night. I placed your broken bear beside you in the cot before retreating to my own bed to see the morning through.

Dear Aiden,

My alarm went off, and I went into autopilot. I swung my legs out from under my rose-patterned sheets, quietly counting my lucky stars for gracing me with a good night's sleep. As I pushed myself out of bed, my hand floated towards my stomach on instinct, caressing you and waking you up, too. I only found my now loose-fitting pyjama top. My legs buckled beneath me, and I crashed to the floor. My hands grabbed at my stomach once more. I was scared I would agitate you by moving so suddenly, yet my hands found nothing for the second time. It was all just air. I ran to the toilet spewing vomit across the carpet and walls as I moved. I vomited on the tiles around the toilet floor and all over the wooden seat. By the time I held my head over the bowl, I had nothing left in me. I brushed my teeth before tiptoeing over the vomit back to my bedroom and began getting ready for work.

They had forgotten to take down the congratulations banner above my desk, and I winced when I saw it. The office manager, Dan, caught my eye and followed it to see what I was gawping at. Working in a marketing agency, we're known for being sticklers for detail, but sometimes it's the errors that sit right under our noses that get overlooked the most.

"Shit, shit, shit. Oh, shit! Barbara, I am so sorry." His hand covered his mouth and the colour drained from his usually rosy cheeks. He shook his head and a few wisps of his brown hair sprung free from the wax that previously held it slicked back. "I told Margaret to take it down yesterday. Oh, God. Shit! I am so sorry."

"It's alright, Dan, I'll do it."

"No, no, honestly, Barb. I'll take it down right now." He patted his tie and buttoned his blazer as if going to his weekly meeting with our investors. "We just, we weren't expecting you back so soon after..." he trailed off. I looked at him, daring him to finish his sentence—daring someone, anyone—to utter aloud what happened and for it to enter reality.

"Dan?" He turned towards me once more and froze, like hot wax hitting a cold surface. "I will take the banner down. Thank you, anyway."

His mouth opened and closed, his full lips smacking together like my grandfather's once did at the kitchen table, the sign of a good meal. He took this as a dismissal and quickly retreated to his office. I could see curious co-workers peeking over computer screens and through cubicle windows. I waved, and most of them blinked out like cat's eyes in the night. I headed towards my desk and that haunting congratulations banner that hung above it. I pulled my chair against the wall and stepped onto it. I willed my hands to remain on the wall and not dash protectively to my shrivelled stomach. I pulled the banner off the wall and folded it neatly and carefully. I was far too aware of every pair of eyes on me. I scratched at the blue-tack for a good five minutes, but it wouldn't come away from the tiny little grooves in the paint.

I felt a firm hand on my back.

"Barbara? Your sister's on her way, I think you should go home."

"Dan, I'm fine. Please, just let me get rid of this tack."

"Barb, there's no tack there. You picked it off about 20 minutes ago."

I looked at my hand. My nail had been filed down to my finger. Blood had started to seep out of a friction burn that looked a lot worse than it felt. This would be our first *oopsy daisy*, Aiden. I held my finger. I kissed it. This would be our first *magic kiss to make it all better*. After our magic kiss, you'll giggle, and I'll pull a packet of jelly cubes from my bag. We'll share one to help the pain go away.

Dan helped me down from my chair and then grabbed my coat and bag, using the same authority he adopts sometimes when the business needs it most. Your bottle of milk fell to the floor and cracked. Lukewarm milk spread and soaked into the grey office carpet. Your rattle fell out too, and the handle snapped off. Your dummy tumbled into carpet dust motes that should have been cleaned up over the weekend by Margaret.

I hit the floor, desperately trying to save all things *you* before reality stole them from me. The milk seemed desperate to seep away from under my nail beds as I tried to scoop it back into the bottle. I wiped your dummy, praying there were no germs on it. I couldn't have my little boy getting a *belly-boo*. Your rattle was in two pieces.

My head snapped towards Dan. "That was the only rattle he's got." I see specks of spit flying through the air like missiles between us. "He was going to be a musician, Dan. He was going to write his first-ever girlfriend a song that I would play back to him on his 21st birthday. Now look what you've done. That was his only rattle."

Dan just stared at me with his mouth shaped like a Cheerio.

"Who's *he*, Barbara?"

"Who's *he*? Who the hell are *you*? He is my son! How dare you speak about him like that? He is my world and you, Dan, are nothing. That was his only rattle!"

Quick footsteps to my right drew my attention away from Dan. Fi was running towards me, across the office.

"Barbara? Sweetie, come on. Come with me, it's alright. We'll get him a new rattle." Fi's hands rested on my pointed finger and brought it back down, away from Dan's face. She began sweeping up your things, carelessly throwing them into my bag. She ushered me out of the office like a boozy, unwanted party guest.

"I swear to God, Fi, if he doesn't replace Aiden's rattle by the end of week, I will give him hell. I will give you hell, Dan!" I screamed over my shoulder, straining my neck to see if he'd heard me. The team just stood and watched as I was hustled into my sister's Fiat.

Dear Aiden,

Aunty Fi took me to our family physician that day. I told her it really wasn't necessary, but we went anyway. For the past week, I've been on medication: 5mg of Diazepam every four hours, and 7.5 mg of Zopiclone each night. I've been forgetful. I'll admit it. I've tried to go back to the agency a few times, but Fi always seems to be on call. Whether she stops me on the way out of the house when I've forgotten she's staying over or she arrives a few minutes later to the office than I do, she's always there. I've spent a lot of time in your nursery. I keep trying to correct the mess I made of your walls, but it all just seems to be getting worse.

The medication has led me to waking up in the strangest of places around the house. Sometimes I'll be by your cot, but once or twice I've woken up in the front room where your presents still sit. I haven't opened them though, Love. Don't worry. I can wait. The medication seems to be making me feel more tired each day, and it's been fogging my memories of you. So, as of today, I'm deciding to bin the rest. Don't tell Aunty Fi.

I'm trying to cling to each memory I have of you. At the agency, I can scrape back to a time when I didn't even know if you were a boy or a girl. You were just called Bump. That's why I keep trying to go back. I've told Dan he can forget about compassionate leave; him letting me into the office is the greatest compassion he could ever show me. Some days Dan calls Fi in the first few minutes of my being there, those are bad days. On other occasions he lets me roam the office a little longer, sometimes up to 20 minutes or more, and I'll have longer to think of you. Alongside your aunty Fi's house and ours, the agency office was where you were discussed most.

I used to float into the office an hour late on my cloud 3,000, and no one would tut or roll their eyes like they did when Sandra was pregnant. Sandra was not a good kind of pregnant. She'd mumble and grumble her way into the office, complaining of back pains and forever cursing her unborn child for the stress and stretch marks he was giving her. Before her pregnancy she had this beautiful thick auburn hair and the brightest of blue eyes. She used to remind me of sunshine in autumn. But when she got pregnant, her hair stuck to the shape of her head, slick with grease and her eyes lost their brilliance.

For us, the office was different. I never complained. Even on those days that I ached or felt sick or when my feet would swell too large for anything other than a pair of clogs, I would still come to work with a smile. It was all worth it when I thought of what I was going to have at the end. One of the team would put the kettle on for me as I eased myself into my chair and we'd all just get on with it. I'd wave away Dan's offers of early maternity leave because I was *glowing*. I was bursting with pride and wanted to share my bump with the world. The girls in the office would rush to my cubicle when they heard me grunt. They knew that meant you were kicking. The men would stand around the perimeter looking on while the girls ran their hands over you. I think a lot of the team used it as an excuse to get away from their desks; phones would be ringing, agitated clients on the other end of the line no doubt. But they would have to wait. Everything would have to wait because you were kicking. In fact, it was the girls who nicknamed you Bump in the first place.

We were in the tearoom. Rachel was supposed to be doing the rounds, bringing mugs of steaming tea and coffee to our desks. We'd be juggling mugs of hot fuel with client calls, trying to bring harmony to haywire and finding calm with each sip we took.

I've always admired Rachel's beauty and her naivety to it. Her light brown curls frame her face, which is void of any blemish or hint of makeup. She has the most indulging green eyes, like the thick of a bush that you just want to fall into. She got braces in the early months I was pregnant and developed a habit of covering her mouth when she speaks. I always thought it was such a shame and I developed my own habit of pulling her hand away every time she did it. She'd roll her eyes and continue speaking, her lips turning up at the corners. Whenever Rachel was doing the rounds, she would claim she couldn't find the tray to carry the mugs, so we'd politely offer to come to her instead. Dan knew about our strategy to get away from our desks. He once made the mistake of trying to break up one of our kitchen rendezvous. He strolled into the kitchen with his blazer buttoned, ready for battle. We'd turned on him like a pack of wolves.

"We'll sit at our desks when we have more comfortable chairs."

"We'll stay in the office longer the second you fix the air conditioning out there."

"Rachel has a family history of arthritis, you want to encourage that, Dan?"

He didn't try to interrupt us again.

All the girls in the office were mums of various ages and had a varied number of kids. I was the last to join the group, and it felt *amazing*. I remember Rachel grabbing my wrist one day as I made my own cup of tea. Her huge green eyes were scanning my face for signs of crazy.

"Barbara, that's salt you're putting in your tea! You know that's salt, right? That's salt."

She didn't really wait for a reply; she just kept uttering salt in that faint Glaswegian accent of hers. It was as if she were confirming it more for herself than me. I just smiled back at her and tipped the rest of the teaspoon into my cup. Rachel let go of my wrist. She took a step back, and her eyes narrowed. She leaned on the counter and, as casually as she could, dared a glance at my stomach. Her eyes flashed back up to mine, and her mouth pressed into a line across her face. I felt my cheeks burning up and broke into a grin.

"I knew it. I knew it! I knew it," she cried.

I tried to sip my tea, but I couldn't stop giggling. Rachel hopped from one foot to the other. I adored the attention.

"How many weeks are you? Do you know if it's a boy or a girl? What cup size are you? Ah, this is too much!" She crammed a few fingers into her mouth and bit down hard still hopping from each foot. Her curls bobbed elaborately with her.

"Oh, can I get the girls? Let me get the girls! Shall I get the girls? I'm getting the girls."

I just laughed, nodded my head, and continued to sip my salted tea. She darted off across the office. Rachel did not do casual well. I turned my back, unable to watch her poor attempt at *discreetly* gathering every girl into the kitchen for an "urgent meeting." By the time Rachel got to Sandra's desk, I think most of them had clocked on that something exciting was happening. They were all doing that same hop Rachel was doing around the office. Like a zombie apocalypse on a packet of sherbet lemons, they ambled towards me.

When the entirety of the female staff had gathered around me, Rachel took it upon herself to hush the group. She turned to me, beaming. I didn't realise I would have to do a speech. The group fell silent—probably for the first time since the agency opened—but they all continued the excited hopping. Various shades of hair swayed from one side to the other in front of me, their faces bobbing in and out of my sight like buoys at sea. I just shook my head, shrugged my shoulders and laughed. I didn't know what to say. I laughed, and then everything got a bit much. I started crying. I couldn't stop crying, but they were happy tears, Aiden. It was all happy. A squeal that I genuinely think has permanently damaged my hearing erupted from those girls. It was like a war cry, but for wolves rather than humans. They smothered me with kisses and awkward side hugs, consciously placed, in risk-to-baby-free areas of my body.

"Watch the bump. WATCH THE BUMP!" Rachel was shouting above the rest of them. Her arms were clearing a small space directly in front of me, just in case you had decided to grow there and my stomach needed the space to expand. She ushered them into a vague order and an avalanche of questions cascaded upon me.

"What's his name?"

"Have you thought of names?"

"Sorry, what's *her* name?"

"When's the baby shower?"

"Is she having a shower?"

"I'll arrange her shower."

"Who says it's a her?"

"Is it a her?"

"Don't call it, *it*."

"Does Dan know?"

"Where's Dan?"

"Who cares about Dan? What cravings are you getting?"

"What cravings did you get?"

"I would murder a bar of Galaxy right now."

"Amen!"

The girls opened up to me like I never thought they would. I was one of them; one of the mums. I heard a loud pop, and the cork of something fizzy dented the ceiling above us. The girls fell silent, and everyone looked to where the noise had come from. A giggling Rachel was cradling a bottle of Cava, left over from a leaving do, and some plastic cups. The girls cackled but quickly pressed their fingers to their lips, following Rachel's lead. They all followed her gaze into the main office.

The rest of the office had gathered around the outskirts of the kitchen. Dan pushed to the front of the crowd and Rachel put the bottle of Cava behind her back.

"What on Earth is going on in here? Rachel?"

I heard a gentle splish-splash of liquid. A bubbly stream could be seen falling between Rachel's legs. The Cava hit the floor and fizzed up with a hiss.

"Dan," one of the other girls said, "we'd like to introduce you to the newest member of our team, Bump." A hand rested on you, on the bump that you were, and on cue, you kicked. That was how you were introduced to the world. Well, that's how you were introduced to my world; with Rachel half hunched over a bubbling bottle of Cava surrounded by women bobbing to music no one could hear, in a kitchen with a hole in the ceiling. It was magical.

I've tried to cling onto these memories as much as I can this past week. I try to relive them every day. Before anyone catches me, I'll stand in the tearoom and try a little salt in my tea.

Dear Aiden,

The attitude in the office has completely changed since I returned med-free. They don't let me take client calls, but I'm still creating campaign decks and reports. The atmosphere is tense, like pulling an elastic band to the point just before it snaps.

Since I stopped the medication, I feel you one hundred times over. My heart literally aches so much sometimes that I need to sit down.

"Are you sure you don't just have indigestion, Barbara?" Dan asked me one day. I looked at him and boiled his face with my eyes. How can anyone be so totally oblivious to heartache?

"Or perhaps it's just a...difficult time of the month?" I scoffed at him. That was the final straw. No more Miss Nice Mum for Dan. If I can't make him understand my pain, then I'll make him feel it in any way I can. I told him where he could stick his time of the month, and he quickly scuttled away. Now, he physically tiptoes past me as he heads for the kitchen. Of course, he doesn't realise his tread is as light as a rhino's and I have the ears of a bat. You would have inherited those, Aiden. The poor sod doesn't stand a chance.

I call him to my desk every time he tries to whisper by. I claim I really need to talk to him on urgent matters. I watch him freeze before his shoulders drop with his heart. That nervous vein starts throbbing in his forehead as he squirms towards me. I relish the power I hold over him.

Mummy is now regarded as the office crazy. I don't know if they've given up calling Fi to pick me up, or if she's stopped answering her phone. Either way, I've completely topped Sandra's divorce. I'm not entirely sure if she's relieved or jealous. She can no longer get away with crying every time she misses a deadline. Moaning the name of her ex-husband doesn't earn her any extension or special favours like it used to. Towards the end of her rule she even went to the extreme of smashing her keyboard over her head when the crocodile tears failed her.

It was all a bit much.

At least she's invited to the Christmas party, though. You see, whenever Mummy asks her colleagues how they are celebrating Christmas, they skirt around the subject like the edge of a cold pool. They start speaking really slow, as if one false step could suck them into my oblivion. Mummy just wants to be able to walk around the office and not see her colleagues turn and walk in the other direction. Mummy's tired of seeing them scuttle or crawl away into nooks and crannies Mummy never knew existed.

You'll be crawling soon, Aidy, and you'll be amazing at it. You'll crawl over to my open arms and I will squeeze you so close to me. I'll squeeze you against my smooth belly, void of bruises and marks, a belly filled to the brim with undying love for you and every one of your little fingers and toes. We'll roll around our front room, filling our home with tears of laughter.

Dear Aiden,

Tinsel has started edging shop windows alongside spray paint snow. The local toy store has a half-price sale on all baby toys. I'll admit it; I've spoilt you rotten. I can't help but think that it will all be worth it. You can't put a price on our first Christmas together. I'm on first name basis with the shopkeeper and all of the assistants at the toy store. They're all asking about you, Aiden. They're asking how old you are, what food you're eating, if you're a "good little boy." I adore it. I adore the attention they give you despite never having met you. Of course, I sing your praises, sing you to the high heavens where those pesky angels are holding onto you, for now. The staff at the toy store love you, Aiden, they really do. I tell them you have a heart of gold, just like the nurse said, and there's plenty to go around. They can't wait to meet you. I've told them they'll just have to.

Dear Aiden,

The Christmas party turned out to be a rather eventful night. I know I wasn't exactly invited. There was an email going around the office inviting people formally. I was roaming around the office the day it got sent out, overlooking the shoulders of my colleagues. Their screens were alive with an animated Santa complete with his sleigh and all eight reindeer: Dasher, Dancer, Prancer, Vixen, Comet, Cupid, Donner and Blitzen. No Rudolph though, not a red nose in sight. I'll tell you all about him at some point, Dear.

The day the invites got sent out, I spent a lot of time in the kitchen. Members of the team would come and go, breaking into strained conversations with me. All of them managed to avoid the hot topic of the Christmas party, though; it was almost admirable. Did they honestly think I wouldn't notice? That crazy Barb would be completely oblivious to the biggest company event of the year? Mistletoe had been put up in doorways; Christmas jumpers from Christmas past were making their annual appearance and of course, in turn, comes our Christmas party.

Sandra came into the kitchen on her phone. She looked up and caught sight of me. *Too late.*

"So, what are you going to wear?" I asked. *You can't turn around now, Dear. Barbara's got you.* She looked left and right, desperately trying to find an excuse to leave, I suppose. The panic in her eyes was almost comical. I leaned on the kitchen counter and watched her sweat. She turned to the fridge and dug deep for the sandwich that she always has wrapped, labelled and sitting in the same place every day.

"Wear to what?"

Really? That's the game we're going to play, Sandra?

I stayed quiet. I walked around behind her, reached under her arm and pulled out her sandwich for her.

"Here you go."

Her face blushed a shade of red I've never seen before; it would look nice on the chimney breast in the front room. I looked at her, my eyebrows raised.

"Thanks," she said, sheepishly, taking the sandwich from me. "I better get back to my desk. I've got a lot on today."

"Sure, Sandra, you do that."

She couldn't have been out of that kitchen quicker if it were on fire. I closed the fridge door for her, sighed and headed back to my desk. I was determined to go to this party whether they wanted me there or not.

I picked out a bottle-green cocktail dress and a chunky golden necklace that used to belong to your grandmother, bless her heart. I spent the day bathing, drinking lots of water and conditioning my hair. I wanted to convince people that I am still fun. That just because I'm a new mum now doesn't mean I can't still go out and party with the rest of them. I found you a sitter from an ad in the local paper. She's a 17-year-old girl who wants to save money for a year of travel once she finishes college. She turned up at seven o'clock sharp and was waved off by her dad, in his car. She was timid, waiting to be invited past the welcome mat. Her braces had cut into her lips and made them slightly swollen. A large pair of red glasses sat on her nose that poked out from under her sunken eyes like the beak of a seagull. Her eyes and hair were an identical brown and she wore her hair back in French plaits on either side. She looked like a practical girl, a plain girl. I liked her. She'd be able to handle you.

"Hi Jackie, come on in. I'll give you a quick tour, my cab's due in about 10 minutes so we have enough time." I led her into the kitchen, pointing at the obvious. "Fridge. Help yourself to anything in there. Patio door." I pointed again. "You don't smoke do you?"

She shook her head vigorously.

"Great, then I don't need to show you how it unlocks." I winked at her and we headed into the hall. I put a palm on the door to the front room. "Front room. TV's in there, maybe you can watch a movie or something? Just keep the volume low so you can listen for Aiden on the baby monitor."

She nodded. *Good girl.* We jogged upstairs.

I lowered my voice. "Bathroom," I whispered, tapping on the door. "Be careful with the flush, it sticks sometimes."

Another brisk nod.

"My room and, last but not least, Aiden's." Your door was pulled tightly shut. "He's fast asleep so we won't risk waking him now. We've had a big day, so he should be out all night, but you never know."

I winked at her again and she smiled. A horn sounded from outside. I jogged into the bathroom, holding my breasts so I didn't have any accidental spillages in front of her. I craned my neck, looking out the window onto the street.

"That's my cab. I gotta go." We headed downstairs and I slipped my heels on. "You have my number if you need anything, right?"

She nodded again. I opened the front door.

"Ms. Bridges?"

"Yes?"

"You look really pretty."

"Thanks, Love." I smiled as I went out the front door and hopped in the cab.

The company had rented a cocktail bar for the night. It's not one I've been to before, but it looked pretty fancy from outside. Lots of fairy lights and dark wood. I pulled up and was rearranging my dress when another cab pulled up behind mine. The girls piled out, already giggly and dressed to the nines. Rachel and Sandra led the way, followed by two other girls from the front desk. They all had their phones out, all smiles and sunshine like an ad for M&S.

"Rachel...hey!" I tottered over to her, breathless, and already regretting my choice of footwear. These heels weren't made for mums.

"Barbara?" Their faces cracked into smiles like ice splintering in warm water.

"The one and only." I smiled, holding my purse in front of me. Rachel shook her head a little, sending those Scottish curls off to dance.

She pulled herself to her senses. "Hey!" She beamed at me and threw her arms out to her sides. I moved in and gave her a small hug.

"I'm pleased you came," she whispered in my ear, and gave me a squeeze. She pulled me at arm's length and looked me up and down. "You look incredible, Barbara. Ladies, let's go!" She took my hand and led me inside. I looked back at Sandra and the other girls. Sandra had pulled out a cigarette.

"You girls head in. I'll be right behind you," she said.

"I like your dress, Sandra," I called out, with perhaps a little bitterness in my voice. Embarrassed, she turned away and attempted to light her cigarette facing the wind. I kicked myself for being so petty, but I couldn't help it. *No more of that Ms. Bridges, tonight is the night to make amends.*

We headed straight for the bar, and Rachel ordered a round of tequila. It was the first time I've drunk since before you, but I wasn't about to turn down my opportunity to re-join the Club again. I got a few second glances from questioning colleagues but most of the office was either more interested in the leggy receptionists behind us or in the bottom of their drink. I was quickly accepted into the night.

More tequila went down, a few cocktails too. Rachel stuck to my hip for the night. I'll always be thankful for that. I kept checking my phone, waiting to hear something from Jackie. No news is good news, I told myself.

Rachel kept grabbing my hand and pulling me onto the dance floor. The fairy lights around us began to merge into one constant glow, and the pain from my shoes ebbed away. My head was as light as spun candy floss. I'd shut my eyes and dance, and when I'd open them, Rachel would be there grinning back at me. She looked fantastic, and her kindness painted her in a light I'd never noticed before. *Thank you, Rachel. Thank you, thank you, thank you.* We were at the bar ordering what I hoped would be our last shot of the night when we were blindsided. A man I'd never seen before appeared on Rachel's left side. He had the eyes of a cat, reflecting every colour from the lights around us. His heavy hand fell on the bar and I was eclipsed. *Don't watch the eclipse, Rachel. It will blind you!*

"Barbara?"

I looked away from the back of the man's head.

"Hi, Dan," I said.

"I'm pleased you could make it," he smiled, and the creases around his eyes set in wax.

"Yeah, thanks for the invite, Dan."

"That's what I wanted to talk to you about, it wasn't my..." I put my hand up to his face, with my palm just inches from his nose.

"Save it, Dan. I don't want to hear it."

"I just want to..."

"Dan, please. Just stop."

Rachel's hand was back in mine and the other was offering a tequila shot. I took it and knocked it back.

"Excuse us, Dan. This is our song," Rachel said. It wasn't our song. Rachel and I didn't have a song. Yet, at this moment in time—and forever and always—it would be our song. Rachel pulled me onto the dance floor once more where we were safe from the rest of the world.

After that point the night is hazy. I remember being with Rachel in the middle of the dance floor and the front desk girls joining us with some hungry looking men in tow.

I remember the bar.

I remember being in the toilets with Rachel, giggling while Sandra threw up in one of the cubicles. Trying to reapply my lipstick and failing. Rachel helping me take it off with a wet paper towel.

I remember the bar...Dan again.

I remember the cab journey home with Rachel sitting in the middle seat next to me, even though there were only the two of us back there. We were laughing so much my cheeks hurt. I dropped my keys on the doorstep. I think I remember Jackie opening the front door. Rachel paying Jackie. Rachel leaving.

I woke up in a ball next to your cot this morning. I grabbed my phone, expecting to see a message from Rachel or one of the other girls. There was nothing, though. No news is good news, right?

24th December

Dear Aiden,

I've tried to call Rachel a few times since the office party. She's proving exceptionally hard to get hold of, especially now that we're on our holidays. Maybe she's gone skiing? I know she loves skiing. That's probably it, she's gone skiing and her phone doesn't have reception. I'll give her a ring after Christmas. I got a text message from Dan the day after the party.

"It was good to see you enjoying yourself again. X"

Thanks, Dan. Of course I'm enjoying myself. Everything is perfect now because I'm one of the mums again.

Our presents are wrapped, each with its own bow and clue on the gift tag. I know you can't read them, but I'll read them to you. Santa's swig of brandy and mince pie is waiting for him by the chimneybreast. It's boarded up, but nothing will stop Santa, don't worry. I think I've counted the carrots out right. There should be enough for each reindeer, so they can continue to deliver presents to all the other well-behaved boys and girls. I've included Rudolph in this, too. I'm too excited to sleep but want nothing else. So here we are, tucked in tight, waiting in the hush of the night for sleep to take us. Waiting for the sound of bells on the rooftop and for hearty laughter to echo through our lazy street.

Dear Aiden,

Merry Christmas, Love. I unplugged the phone last night. I so want this Christmas to be special...to be something that will stay with us for life. I couldn't hold back an ear-to-ear smile as we crept down the stairs this morning.

"Santa?" I called out, halfway down the stairs. "Santa?" I was laughing. This was so perfect. This is everything I'd dreamt of since you were just Bump. "Santa, are you there?"

The coast was clear, and we bustled our way into the front room to a host of presents. I was halfway through unwrapping a new set of bath toys when Fi let herself in.

I sighed. *We need to get those locks changed, don't we, Aiden?*

"Barbara? Merry Christmas! Where are you? Barbara?"

I jumped to my feet, throwing hundreds of pounds of toys behind the sofa. I frantically shoved wrapping paper under the cushions. Fi was at the door, watching it all.

"Barbara, you can't be serious?"

I studied the scraps of wrapping paper on the floor. I'd missed quite a bit.

"Barbara, put your coat on. There's something I want you to see."

I was confused. Why was she dragging me away from our perfect Christmas? We left your presents and headed outside. The air bit at my cheeks and snow drifted in heavy, clumsy clusters that refused to settle. I climbed into Fi's Fiat and watched as children on new skates and scooters whizzed by my window. I watched them wave to their parents, daring to take their eyes off the pavement just for a split second to make sure their audiences were still entertained. I witnessed parents laughing together, taking photos over mugs of hot chocolate. I'll make hot chocolate next year.

"Here we are. Follow me, Barb."

I climbed out of the car and the crisp, slightly frozen grass crunched underfoot. The snow had stopped. Under my coat, I was still in my slippers and bathrobe, and the breeze snapped at my ankles. Fi stopped in front of me, and I almost bumped into her, waving a half-hearted hand in front of my belly. The instinct to protect my bump was fading now. She pulled me to her side and held me there as I read what was in front of us.

"Aiden Bridges
A child so precious, so beautiful, so bold.
The angels called him straight away
To share his heart of gold."

The grave was covered with presents, Christmas cards, and flowers.

"You need to see this, Sis. You need to accept that this is where Aiden sleeps now." I lowered myself to my knees hearing Fi's knees crack as she knelt beside me. We began to open your presents together and read your cards.

Once everything was opened, Fi gave my shoulder an awkward pat, pat, pat. She pulled one final present out of her coat pocket and gave it to me.

"Thank you, Fi. I'll get home myself. Go and see your kids."

I stayed there for the rest of the day arranging your presents around you. Me and you—you and me—against the world. Visitors came, passed short greetings on to loved ones six feet under and then left. I picked up Fi's present. The shape gave it away, and as I picked it up the sound of rain rang through the air. I unwrapped your new rattle and twirled it around in my hands. Sorry it took me so long, Love.

I dug a little way, not caring about the mud caking under my nails. I laid the rattle to rest and let you play with it through the night as tears cascaded down my cheeks.

Dear Aiden,

The psychiatric ward is not the first place I'd think of spending a typical Thursday afternoon, sipping scalding hot coffee, and being watched by various white coat-clad hawks. Yet, here I am. They've wrestled me into this horrific green petal gown with no back. It's breezy in here, Aiden, and Mummy's getting a chilly bot-bot.

"Ms. Bridges?"

A voice that I can only describe as chocolate floated over my thoughts.

I looked up, and my vision clouded.

"That is I."

Sounding like I was in a Brontë novel, I flushed at the most symmetrically beautiful man my eyes have ever had the pleasure of indulging in. The doctor must have been a little over six foot, with beautifully clear skin, the deepest oak brown eyes, and a smile that could outshine the sun. And his hair, Aiden! My God, it was various wisps of auburn that caught the cold glare of the hospital lights and reflected back a rich gold aura that said, *Hi, I'm a Demigod.* I should have been attracted to him, Aiden. I should have blushed and giggled with that laugh I practised for hours when younger. But all I could think was:

One day, I want my Aiden to look like you.

I want my Aiden to have the girls swooning over him, just like you do.

I want their knees to tremble as Aiden breezes by in his lab coat, just like you do.

"Could you follow me please, Ms. Bridges?"

In that one sentence, I managed to consume precisely 2,317 calories of pure Demigod and sweet Mother of Mary, I still craved more. I prayed he would lead me to the heavens. I prayed that he'd turn around when we were on fluffy-white clouds laced with gold and say:

Surprise, Mum. Haven't I grown up fast?

"Certainly, Doctor...?" My voice went up an octave as I finished my question. It was supposed to just raise a note, but my craving got the better of me. I crumbled like the sweet chocolate chip cookie he was made of.

My fingers were crossed too tightly behind my back, hoping against hope he would introduce himself to me as Dr. Bridges. I'd take it as a sign that somewhere, somehow, you were living on; that those angels who snatched you from me had reintroduced you into the life of someone who needed you more, somewhere you were making a family so blissfully happy it hurts.

"Dr. Abbott, but you can call me whatever you like." He smiled, and his eyes were a log fire on a winter's day, full of comfort and warmth.

My heart, originally soaring over clouds of chocolate gold, plummeted like rain drops as heavy as golf balls and sank in an ocean of *what the fuck was I thinking.* I was struck by the realization of how deluded I'd allowed myself to become. I snatched up our baby carrier, threw away the now warm coffee and followed Dr. Abbott into his not quite, but almost, perfect office.

"Please," Dr. Abbott gestured towards a seat that looked a lot less plush alongside his. With reluctance, I sat.

I took in the warm chestnut panelled walls of his office, the royal greens alongside golds and silvers that were fit for the birth of Christ. I was petrified; the more luxurious the room, the higher up the person who dwells within it. The higher up the person a patient sees implies the extent of the damage in need of treatment. *Shit.* My eyes glazed over when I saw pristine family photos lining his desk. I'll learn from my mistakes for next time, Aiden. I won't let you out of my sight. As soon as those misleading angels grace you on this Earth, I'll clasp you to me and hold you so tight they'll have to pry you from my arms with tools forged from titanium.

"Now then, do you know why you're with us today, Ms. Bridges?"

"No."

"Your GP referred you."

A pause.

"After a friend of yours confirmed that you hired a babysitter for your child that is no longer with us."

"Oh."

"Are there any other reasons you can think of as to why you're here, Ms. Bridges?"

"No."

"Oh."

The look that Dr. Demigod gave me after his coral pink lips created the perfect "oh" was meant to convey *where do we start?*

I sighed.

He sighed.

He got out a file thicker than *The Oxford English Dictionary* from his drawer.

I got out a pack of tissues and some jelly cubes.

Looks like I'm in for more than I thought. This is going to take a while.

Saying that those four hours were hideous is an understatement. Dr. Abbott started with your grave:

> *"Aiden Bridges,*
> *A child so precious, so beautiful, so bold.*
> *The Angels called him straight away*
> *To share his heart of gold."*

Tears welled up in my tired eyes. My hands chased each other to the point where my nine-month stomach once reached; I caressed what was once you. Dr. Abbott watched this, his pen scribbling in what I imagined to be flawless handwriting.

"You have no right to repeat those words. You don't know him, no one on this Earth knows him. None of you have any right." I managed to keep my voice level.

"Barbara, I want us to get to the bottom of your..." *Go on*, I thought. *Diagnose me. Put a label on my inability to hold onto my child. Brand me with the rest of them; put me in a jar for observation on the shelf.*

"...your condition."

Let your med students take notes on my instability, watch them laugh at me over lunch across steaming cups of tea as they text their babysitters.

"The only way we are going to get to the bottom of this is if we approach it head on. We need to accept Aiden's death."

Cue the camera crew.

"If we accept his passing, we can then look at the trauma it has caused and work towards a solution..."

Congratulations, Barbara Bridges, you've survived our longest pranking in history!

"...that will eventually help you to move on with your..."

Oh, you guys! You got me, you little scamps. Where's my little boy then? Where are you hiding him? Come back to me, Aiden.

"What's your first name, Dr. Abbott?"

"James." *Beautiful.*

"Have you ever lost a child, James?"

"I think we're not quite grasping the subject here..."

"*Have* you ever lost a child, James?"

He shifted his weight from his left to right butt cheek.

"No, no I haven't."

"Well, then. With all due respect James, with all your qualifications: A-levels, O-levels, degrees and doctorates, you have absolutely zero experience in my position. No amount of education will ever help you to understand that."

"Barbara..."

"Oh, don't you Barbara me. You sound exactly like the rest of them. I've had enough Barbara-ing for a lifetime, James."

"Ms. Bridges calm down, please. Let's start from Boxing Day. I am told your sister, Fiona..."

"Fi."

"Fi, sorry, found you at your son's grave. There were reports from neighbouring houses of odd noises being heard at various hours throughout night. Had you stayed there since Christmas Day, Barbara?"

"My son's a musician, James. He plays the most beautiful music you will ever hear." I couldn't help telling him you were a musician. He had opened up all these poorly patched together holes. He had hacked his way through my rib cage and taken a carving knife to my heartstrings. Our music was weeping, Aiden. It was so beautiful to hear, so clear. The sound of your rattle filled my ears, poured out of my eyes and danced its way between us.

"And one day, James, he'll be a poet. For a brief time, he'll learn to play the drums, but that will be a phase. After that he'll pick up an acoustic guitar and never look back. He'll fly through his secondary school exams, go to college, find the woman who will one day be his wife, and the two of them will study medicine."

"Barbara, please..."

"He'll take a gap year after that, claiming he wants to 'find himself.' It'll be the hardest thing I'll ever have to do, letting him go. But I'll know he's old enough to fly the nest. I'll realise his wingspan is great enough to soar the world. In a year, he'll come back to me, having saved so many lives in South India. He'll come back and surprise me for my birthday. He'll be on the board of a notable charity. He'll run the marathon, and I'll wait with his girlfriend at the finish line. There he'll propose to her, and I'll cry my weight in salty tears even though I knew about it all along."

"Barbara, we are getting ahead of ourselves."

"I'll help to prepare his wedding day. I'll take his fiancé shopping for a dress. We'll be like sisters, getting on like we've known each other our entire lives because my son knows how to pick 'em."

"Boxing Day, Barbara, tell me about Boxing Day."

"On Boxing Day, she'll announce that she is pregnant with a little girl. No. She is pregnant with twins. I'll make jokes about being such a young grandmother."

"Barbara, I didn't want to do this, honestly I didn't, but I need to bring you back to Earth."

"I'll offer to babysit every day of the week all while pretending I'm sick of it. I'll never be able to resist the joy of being asked and being trusted with such precious little lives."

"On Boxing Day, you were found unconscious because of what was latter classified as sleep deprivation, post-traumatic stress, and depression."

"They'll keep me up all day long, but those two will keep me young."

"An ambulance was called, and when it arrived on the scene you woke. You hit a medic in the face, screaming that he was a thief, before sprinting away across the graves."

"And at night they'll sleep like angels. They'll have little smiles on their faces while their hands twitch their way through dizzy dreams. I'll just sit and watch them until Aiden and his wife arrive home from their art exhibition on South Bank."

"Barbara, you fell to the ground and started digging up earth, claiming Aiden needed to be woken up or he wouldn't sleep that night. That day you were hospitalised, suffering from severe trauma and self-inflicted head and abdomen injuries."

"Aiden would hug me in those big arms of his and thank me for being there for him. He'd thank me for being the most perfect mother anyone could wish for. On New Year's Eve, each year, I will bake them all a cake. Not a Christmas cake because none of them like raisins, but I'll bake them a lemon drizzle, something for them to enjoy on New Year's Day."

"January 5th, you were released and placed in the immediate and direct care of your sister, Fi."

"Fi and I will help sort through the hundreds of Christmas gifts the twins will receive. We'll dress them in the cutest little outfits speckled with matching stripes and spots."

"Barbara, are you remembering any of this? I need you to listen to me, Barbara. Aiden is dead."

"Oh?"

"We need to come to terms with that."

"Aiden? My Aiden? He plays the most beautiful music, James. Just listen. Oh, it's so glorious, isn't it?"

"Aiden is dead, Barbara."

"Where is he, James?"

"Aiden?"

"No, you imbecile! The host, the guy running this sad excuse for a comedy. Where is he hiding? When is this game going to be over? Where have you hidden the cameras?"

At this point, Poppet, I lumbered out of that plastic chair of mine. There's no other way of saying this—I quite simply tore Dr. James' office apart. I decided the curtains didn't match the floor, so they had to go. Then the floor didn't match the view from the window, so up came the rug. I vaguely remember that devil reaching for a phone I'd never noticed before, but then the medical books caught my eye. They weren't in alphabetical order, so out they came. A flurry of white coats flocked around me like the gulls at Southend on Sea.

I blacked out, and when I woke your music had been silenced and a group of nurses were looking down on me. I felt numb, not entirely sure if that was the doing of whatever had been rammed into my arm or because, once more, you had been taken from me.

Let's run away from here, Aiden. Let's run away from it all. We don't need doctors in fancy offices telling us how we should or shouldn't act. We don't need to wait around for our friends to whisper behind our backs. As soon as I'm out of this place, I'll pack our things and we'll move away. There's still hope for us yet. We can start afresh.

I was manhandled into a hospital bed, and a nurse was placed to watch over me. She picked up a magazine with some sob story on the front cover of a woman who couldn't stop losing weight. I rolled my eyes and tutted away at her but either she's hard of hearing or she was pretending to ignore me. Her eyes were sharp though. I tried to slip out of the bed once. I was just so desperate to get out of there. I thought that perhaps I could convince one of the patients to cover for me. I had visions of running down the corridor, fellow inmates pushing trolleys and throwing trays of sloppy food in the path of the hospital attendees chasing after me. I pictured reaching the escalator at the end of the corridor, pressing the button and giving the nurses the finger as the door closed amid the encouraging cheers and shrieks of my fellow hospital companions.

"Don't make me run," the nurse mumbled the second my toes touched the floor. Her eyes were still on her magazine. I tutted once more and swung my legs back onto the bed.

"You can't keep me here against my will, you know? I know my rights."

"We can, but we won't." She continued with her article. "Your sister is on her way. We need the bed."

Brilliant.

Just as the nurse finished her sentence, Fi marched into the room with a new doctor at her side. She prickled, like a conker in autumn.

"Get up, we're going home." I looked towards the nurse.

Was it going to be this easy?

I swung my legs out of bed, waiting for the nurse to object, but her head stayed in her magazine. The doctor Fi came in with had picked up the clipboard at the bottom of my bed and was scribbling away. Fi hooked her arm under my elbow. I was right, *prickly.* I started to collect my things, but Fi snatched them from me and rammed them into a bag. We left the ward.

Her Fiat needed a wash.

"What about Dr. James? I haven't finished telling him about what will accompany the lemon drizzle cake. I haven't told him our strategy for the DFS January sales." Fi just shook her head, took my preposterous bag of drugs out of my hands, and threw it on the back seat. I realised what I was saying. My hand shot to my mouth, physically clamping it shut as, once again, my body functioned before my brain had a chance. I allowed myself to be ushered into the dirty Fiat, kicking aside empty boxes of McDonald's apple pies.

Fi slid in next to me, pulled across her belt, jammed her keys into the ignition, reached out to turn down the radio, and exhaled one, long, yoga breath. The windscreen fogged, and her hand dropped from the volume button to the gear stick. She looked straight ahead.

"I'm not sure how much longer I can do this, Barbara. You just...you just require so much from me, and there's only so much..." She trailed off, perhaps realising that her stream of conscious was being uttered aloud to someone in no position to think of anyone but herself.

She lit a cigarette and rolled down the window an inch or two. She started the car, swung out of the car park, and silence engulfed us for the rest of the journey.

Dear Aiden,

Fi dropped me home that day then disappeared under a magician's cloth. I haven't seen her since. It's like the magician only had so much energy and now can't undo his spell. I've called her over and over but still no luck. I took the bus to her place earlier today. I waited on the doorstep for a good three hours, occasionally knocking on the door and peering through the windows. I think a neighbour reported me because the police "happened to be passing by" and ushered me on.

I meandered along every road we will one day walk together. Images of Dr. James' office kept clouding my vision. I found myself hitting one ear as if the images could be dislodged and slip out of the other like sand. I hit myself so hard whilst strolling past Krishna's tobacco store that I stumbled into the road. An approaching car blasted its horn and swerved to the other side of the road. The passenger was screaming obscenities at me over blaring music, but none of it so much as made a dent on the images of Dr. James' office. White coats, needles and name badges fluttered across the front of my mind like the wings of birds in flight.

At least Mummy's got her magic medicine now to make everything better. Dr. Abbott assured me that these ones won't make me feel fuzzy. As soon as I opened the boxes, I realised how wrong they'd got the branding. They coloured each pill with bright pinks, greens and blues. They looked like all sorts of liquorice. Of course, I thought of you. I imagined your curious little hands grabbing them off the work surface as I carried you into the kitchen. I imagined me pulling your hand away from your mouth, thinking you had started that awful habit of sucking your thumb. I imagined seeing the remaining specks of the pills caught in your fingernails. The thought brings tears to my eyes. They really shouldn't make them so bright. Perhaps I'll write a letter.

"S'cuse me, Miss." I stepped to the side of the pavement to let a boy, who must have been around 12, speed past me on his scooter. He grazed the bush as he did so because the pavement wasn't wide enough for the two of us. Still, I'd rather that than see him scoot in the road. He ducked under a stray branch, and his red-check beanie was pinched from his head. A great mass of brown curly hair let loose in the wind. I ran through what I should do in my head:

Hey, Kid!

No, that wouldn't work. I didn't live in New York, and I am not on film.

Boy! Your hat!

No, no, that wouldn't do either. I'm not young enough to pull that off.

Son! I choked.

Images of you on that scooter flooded my head, and I swiftly got to knocking them out and into the road. I looked back up and the boy was just turning the corner onto Manford Way. I took a quick look around to see if anyone had witnessed my monstrous attempt at socialising, but there was not a soul in sight. I picked up the hat and stuffed it into my coat pocket. It seemed a shame to leave it out there in the elements. I hastened my pace and headed in the same direction as the mop-haired boy.

I circled the block three times. Part of me was hoping to bump into the boy again. Part of me was just happy to have some kind of purpose.

People don't really go for walks these days. Not on their own, and not without purpose. Maybe I should get a dog, or at least some shopping bags to make it look as if I have a place to go or have just come from somewhere.

I finally returned to our road just as the sun, woven in pastel-pink candy floss clouds, was dipping into London's horizon. I clutched the boy's hat in my pocket as tightly as I once held that pregnancy test all those months ago. With a final glance towards each end of the empty street, I turned into our front garden, slipped the key in the door and retreated inside.

I let out a sigh of relief as I heard the lock click behind me. I pulled the boy's hat out of my pocket. Had I just stolen it? I held the hat to my chest. I felt so alive. I put it at arm's length, inspecting my treasure. It had dark red-check squares on black cotton, almost like a kilt. The fabric was thick. I'm surprised he didn't notice as soon as the wind rushed its way through his brown locks. Or, perhaps he did? Perhaps he's retracing his steps right this moment. Perhaps someone witnessed me and is describing me to him, pointing in the direction I'd headed. The thought of that thrills me even more. I ran my fingers along the stitching and followed it to the hat's interior and fumbled with a silk label. Looking down I notice a fine red pen scrawled over the washing instructions:

Oliver Harp
19 Arweneck Avenue

Well, it's a pleasure to meet you, Oliver.

Dear Aiden,

Arweneck Avenue is the kind of street I hope to live on one day. It isn't a huge leap from where we are now. It is just enough that I'd want to invite old neighbours from previous towns over for dinner. It has 58 terrace houses on it, each with red brick, different coloured doors, and different-sized porches. Some porches are as bare as a summer's sky, and others are a jungle-run of shoes and assorted coats. One day, we'll have a porch, Aiden. Some of the doors have rustic knockers on them with faces of bronze lions or human hands balled into a fist.

Cars can only go as far as houses 15 and 16 from one end of the street; on the other end, they can only reach houses 46 and 47. This is because there's a great square of grass in the middle of the street. It's the only street like it in the area (as far as I know). The grass has the obligatory *NO BALL GAMES* sign sitting on top of a sorry-looking post that is crippled over like a villain from a fairy-tale.

Oliver's house is perfect. It has a waist-high hedge on either side of a brown-red gate. The paintwork is flaking away like weathered bark from a willow tree. Oddly shaped stepping stones lead to an almost empty porch, save for a coconut wind chime in the window. Two pairs of muddy football boots keep each other company on the front step and both look sodden wet. The grass around the stepping stones hasn't been cut in a while and is starting to reclaim the edges of the path. Daisies speckle the grass. Their yellow and white tips look like flecks of paint on a green canvas. The ground floor at the front of the house has been extended into the front garden by a metre or so. The brickwork is a slightly lighter shade of red compared to the weather-worn bricks behind it. The ground floor has three sets of windows.

My favourite window looks directly into the dining room. It doesn't have any blinds or shutters. I imagine at night you can see a smiling and laughing family passing hot plates of organic food around the table like something out of a film. Despite it being January, I picture them wearing those Christmas hats you get in crackers. I picture a grandfather; he's still sprightly but every time he coughs, the parents exchange a quick, worried look. I picture Oliver's curly brown hair catching the glow of fairy lights, which are up all year round, exposing tones of red in his hair. Yes, Oliver's house is quite beautiful.

Dear Aiden,

I've taken to a habit of walking past Oliver's house once a day, grasping onto his hat in my pocket. It's my armour in case anyone asks questions about my sudden recurrence down a street on which I do not live. I'm not entirely sure what I'm hoping for or aiming to achieve. I suppose with his hat I've been given a new direction, scrap that, I've been given direction, *period*. A couple of times I've debated hopping across those stepping stones to the front porch. Whoever answers the chime of the bell I'd gracefully retrieve Oliver's hat out of my pocket. I'd smile at them, a full-teeth smile that would crinkle my eyes and exclaim: "I believe this belongs to you."

On one occasion, I actually came close to doing it. I took a deep breath and seized to a halt by the gate. I even turned towards the house, but the lights in the dining room were flicked on, and my feet carried me down the road before my brain had a chance to agree. Now, I've finally found the courage to knock on the glass door of the porch. It has been a little over two weeks since Oliver whizzed past me on his scooter. Is it too late to bring a hat back into his life he has probably already grieved for and managed to let go? I couldn't do that to him now.

I still haven't heard anything from Aunty Fi. I guess she'll come back to me when she's ready. When we were younger, we used to argue a lot. We were both so stubborn and usually refused to admit anything was our fault. We'd argue, and then go sulk in our rooms, sucking our thumbs. We'd miss each other in minutes. Fi only ever seemed to return to me when I was on my feet, heading to my door and ready to offer apologies. I'd be at my door just as there would be a gentle knock from the other side. Fi, would see herself in, red-eyed and hair astray. I'd take her into my arms and we'd cuddle without passing a word between us. We'd soon go back to playing just as we had before, our arms scarred with nail marks from the other, our thumbs pruned but our tears dried and forgotten.

The medication from the hospital is helping me manage the days going by. I know Fi will come back, when I'm ready, she'll come knocking. I just hope I can take her into my arms again. I hope that the scars she's left this time around are no more than skin deep.

Dear Aiden,

I turned onto Arweneck Avenue yesterday to see a group of boys playing out on the grass. Every time one of the boys kicked the football, a small cluster of leaves followed. I stopped, watching the late winter fireworks play out in front of me. My grip around Oliver's hat tightened in my pocket. I started scanning faces, squinting at the boys. I pulled a pack of strawberry jelly from my pocket and tore myself a cube. The ball was kicked too hard, too many leaves were sent into the air, a flurry of copper browns and lipstick reds. I heard the thud of metal as the ball hit a nearby car, and a hushed "ooh" echoed between the boys. They exchanged wary glances to on-looking windows. I looked too, guiltily sharing their suspense. I swallowed the jelly cube while scanning windows. I eventually looked back to the boys and their eyes were on me. The ball was at my feet. Oh God, Aiden. The ball was at my feet! I looked from the ball to the expectant faces, and then from the faces to the ball. One of the boys' hands shot up in the air.

"S'CUSE ME! MISS?"

Oliver?

A thick, east London accent rang through the air. *Oliver!* He was jogging towards me—his hair leaping up and down with his stride, waving me back to Earth. I went to kick the ball in his direction, and then thought better of it. I turned on my heels and fled back in the direction I'd come. But not before our eyes met. He looked confused, and I know I looked panicked. Aiden, I couldn't have looked guiltier if I'd tried. His brilliant, green eyes managed to survey my face for a second before I turned away.

I tried to put myself into his football boots. What conclusion would I draw if a strange woman had been watching me play football, had gone to kick the ball to me, and then panicked and ran away like a schoolgirl? Hopefully he'll think nothing of it. Hopefully he'll dismiss it and just be pleased that I didn't tell him off for playing ball games on what was obviously supposed to be a ball-free green. I can't shake the look he'd given me though, Aiden. I felt his eyes on my back for the rest of the journey home. Of course, I know he wasn't following me. I know that as soon as he had his ball, he turned and kicked it back to his friends. I heard the thud as his boot connected with the ball and pictured the rush of leaves follow in its wake. I risked one last look back at him over my shoulder. The boys were exactly as they had been, undisturbed by the series of events that had just passed them by. If only all events were that easily overcome.

Part of me wanted him to forget me. Life on Arweneck Avenue would be easier that way. But part of me secretly wanted him to remember me, to ponder over me. Him thinking about me excites me. I could be at the forefront of his mind. Even if he were doing something else, forcing down his serving of greens or brushing his teeth before bed. The thought of my face reoccurring in his mind thrills me and spurs me to see him again. I must see him again, Honey. He has a pull on me that I can't quite explain. I suppose I'm just intrigued. I have an insight into his life now, an invitation to delve in and witness the world through his eyes. The hat isn't enough, Honey. I want to know more. I need to know more.

Dear Aiden,

Oliver's eyes were in my dreams. Everyone I walked past had them and everyone gave me that same confused look. The imprint of those huge oval eyes on the backs of my eyelids transferred onto my darkness and swamped my walls. I woke up in fear but also excitement, a rush of adrenaline flooding my veins and making it hard to drift back off into any deep sleep. I slept sporadically into the early hours of the morning with scenarios of Oliver weaving through my mind. I finally woke late in the afternoon, a stream of sunlight prying my eyes open.

I can't keep returning to Oliver's street without reason. Yet, I know I'm not quite done with Oliver Harp in my life just yet. I got out of bed and headed downstairs. I fished out his hat from my coat pocket and have brought it with me into the kitchen. I've laid the hat on the table and sat opposite. Like an awkward dinner date, we stare at each other in silence. I can faintly hear a siren echoing outside, a dog barking, someone shouting.

A dog barking.

That's it, that's exactly it. Dog walkers have purpose. No one questions a dog walker for being somewhere they're not supposed to be. We're not going back to Arweneck Avenue for the rest of the week, Love. We're going to find a dog instead.

Dear Aiden,

Let me introduce you to the newest member of our family. Her name is Saada, and she is stunning. She's a—brace yourself for this—Nova Scotia Duck Tolling Retriever. She has a gorgeous white and gold coat with a white belly and a white stripe down the centre of her face. The glorious gold makes her look like she's wearing a gold-plated shell. Her two front paws are white, like she's wearing the Queen's gloves. I found her at Canning Town Rescue Centre. Why anyone would abandon such a beautiful dog is beyond me.

The nice lady at the centre told me Saada is about four years old and will need to be walked plenty. She also said Saada is great with children. I told her that suits us perfectly and that we would welcome Saada into our lives with open arms. I think we found each other at the right time. Saada needs us and we need her.

She's so well behaved, Honey! I can take her off her lead, and she'll just potter along by my side. Occasionally, she'll run off to inspect a tree or sniff at a stained lamppost, but other than that, she's by my side. I can't wait to introduce the two of you.

It took a while for Saada to settle into her new home. She's calm, but she's also exceptionally inquisitive. The front room has been a no-go for her as she's beginning to moult her winter coat. I also haven't returned to your room since the night of the Christmas party, so your door has been sealed off as well. She's a persistent pooch though, and on more than one occasion, I've caught her pawing at each door, desperate to see inside.

I've taken her for lots of walks. We've been across the forest where I introduced her to the game of fetch. It was hardly a challenge for her. I have a lousy throwing arm, and she has enough energy for the both of us. Still, she enjoys it nonetheless.

I turned into Arweneck Avenue earlier today for the first time with Saada at my side. She stopped with me and together we scanned the empty street. It was around 10 in the morning; too late for the nine-to-fivers and too early for the late risers. I couldn't help but grind to a halt outside Oliver's house and Saada's tail began to wag. She kept looking from the gate to me. I knew no one would be home at this time of day. Presumably, Oliver would have left for school by now, and his parents at work. Before I knew what I was doing, I'd opened the little gate and pushed it forward. The hinges creaked just as I'd imagined they would.

This past week we've been playing a lot of fetch around the house. I'll point at something, and Saada will go and grab it for me. Every now and again she'll decide that she likes the object more than I ever could. I'll find bits of it scattered around the house for days. I'm still finding parts of the slippers that Fi got me last Christmas. But normally, she's pretty good at the game.

"Go fetch, Saada." I pointed at what I wanted. Saada sprinted into the front garden. The thrill of what we were doing must have excited her, too. She grabbed one of the football boots in her mouth, clenched her jaw and sprinted back. I grabbed the boot from her teeth and slipped it into my shopping bag, not daring to look around, and I hustled Saada on. Of course, the new route we had to take did not help my nerves. I tried to walk like my only intention was to give my dog fresh air and exercise. It was difficult. Sweat beads began to prickle my forehead despite the breeze of the day. I put Saada back on her leash and was constantly gripping it too tight or too loose. I didn't know how to manage the tension in my arms. The shopping bag with Oliver's boot in it felt so heavy, like I was carrying our food for the week.

Saada was over-excited the entire journey home. I gave her a few sharp tugs on the lead when she pulled too hard, but only because it gave me something to do. I tried talking to her, mothering her, but I kept getting choked up at the motherly tone I was using even though I swore I never would. The rest of our journey continued in silence; it was probably 10 minutes longer than it needed to be and 10 minutes longer than what Saada was used to. If I put my mind to it, I could have got us back a lot quicker, but I had this overwhelming feeling we were being watched, that somehow, we had been followed from Arweneck Avenue. So, I over-compensated and doubled Saada's walk. It's okay. We'll do a smaller one tomorrow.

It was only once we got back to the house that I realised we forgot to shut the gate. Scenarios began playing through my head. A football boot missing. The police being called. A crime team coming in. The garden being dusted for fingerprints. Mine found on the gate. Saada's hairs being picked out between the last of the daisies. A knock at my door. The police on the doorstep.

I shook the absurd images from my head and brought the shopping bag into the kitchen. I went to put the bag down on the table until my superstitions took hold of me. *Never place new shoes on the table.* Remember that, Sweet Pea. It'll do you no harm and may do you good. I put my shopping bag on the chair and pulled out the goods. I shouldn't really have filled the bag with my best cardigan, but I needed to bulk it up a bit. The muddy boot had left little brown stains on a once coffee cream cardigan, oh well.

Welcome home, Oliver.

I brought the boot to the kitchen window, allowing the natural light to illuminate it in all its glory. The boot was still damp; perhaps they never dried because they were constantly in use. I ran my fingers along the stitching and pictured Oliver pulling his laces as tightly as he could. I pictured myself helping him pull them that little bit tighter before his final game in the Sunday little league. I'll cheer him on at the sidelines alongside the other mums. We'll share flasks of hot chocolate on the colder days and glasses of Pimms throughout the summer months. I let my fingers run inside the boot and checked the size: One. Size one? Oliver must be around 12 years old. There's no way his boot could be this size. I flipped the boot over but saw nothing. I looked on the inside rim, still nothing. I pulled the tongue of the shoe out from in between the laces and sure enough there was that same red scrawl:

Rupert Harp
19 Arweneck Avenue

Well, this just gets better and better. Nice to meet you, Rupert. Welcome to the family.

Dear Aiden,

Saada and I have been walking Arweneck Avenue every day, giving our cheery "good mornings" to fellow dog walkers. We nod our greetings to the postman as I call Saada to my side to let him pass. It's all become very mundane very quickly.

The boots were moved into the porch. I can see them through the glass door, locked up all snug beside the faded welcome mat that I hadn't noticed before. Rupert's other boot sat alongside his brother's for a few days after my crime until it was finally replaced by a shiny green pair. A few days after that Oliver's set were replaced with the same green pair in, what I assume to be, a bigger size. His old pair was slung into the front garden. I wasn't sure whether this was a trick. It looked like the boots were feeding the pigeons, scattered in the garden like breadcrumbs.

The first day I saw them, I had to stop myself from opening the gate and sending Saada in all over again. The drive to steal is so strong. I want those boots. I need them. I know they are Oliver's and that this time I will not be disappointed. But so far, I have refrained. I'll leave them for a few more weeks, until they blend better with the brown green canvas. I'll let the family forget about them, and then I'll let Saada loose once more.

Taking these boots is going to be a much riskier operation. I've begun to walk Saada past the house at different times on different days to try to understand the family's routine. I've learnt that Oliver leaves for school every morning at 8:05. He meets his two friends, I think one of them is called Samuel, on the green. The three of them stand there chatting for a while before Oliver's parents, with Rupert in tow, rush outside and usher them on. Oliver's father isn't what I expected. He has a receding, strawberry blonde hairline and pale, freckled skin. He wears glasses on the end of his nose and is rather stout. He isn't old, but he comes across as though he were once old before his time. Oliver's mother, on the other hand, is perfect in every way. She is tall and slim with those same full green eyes and thick, dark, curly hair that sits happily on her shoulders. She never wears heels, which I like, yet she still stands almost half a foot above Oliver's father. The two of them, together, make an odd coupling, but apparently, opposites attract. Anyway, Aiden, it looks as though Oliver got most of his mother's genes, save for the height.

Oliver's younger brother, Rupert, is a sweetheart. He *does* follow in his father's footsteps, but it is all rather becoming on him. He has the same strawberry blonde sweep of hair on top of a freckled face, a tiny button nose and his mother's glorious green eyes. Rupert has the same style glasses as his father, but he will always be holding them in his hands until one of his parents tells him otherwise. I think his eyesight is pretty bad, though. On one particularly cold morning, Rupert came out of the house first. He had his glasses in one hand and his school bag slung over his left shoulder. Rupert managed to trip over one of the old football boots, which—to my pleasure—he kicked into the hedge. After that stumble, he carried on towards the gate. Saada and

I couldn't help but look on. He stubbed his toe on a dislodged stepping stone that I've noticed every other family member consciously steps over to stop themselves from coming to the same fate. After the stubbed toe, he stumbled into the gate, and then gave up for a moment. He pulled out an inhaler and took a few sharp intakes. Panting for breath, he opened up his glasses, and slipped them into place on his button nose. He inspected the damage, leaning on the bush at first but he quickly started sinking into it. He changed tactics and leant on the gate instead. Saada and I watched as he pulled off his shoe and sock, adjusting his glasses like scientists do in the movies to get a better look at his toe. His parents came rushing out the door, flustered, buttoning coats, seeing Rupert, and seeing me.

"Hello." Oliver's mother was looking right at me. Not realising, I'd crossed the green and drawn to a halt where their neighbour's fence ends and their hedge begins. I was smiling. I was just standing there, smiling at Rupert and his throbbing toe.

"I...um..." I patted my sides and pushed my hands deep into my coat pockets. "I believe this belongs to you." It didn't come out quite how I'd envisioned. I had to draw a raspy breath half way through the sentence, and my throat had all but swollen up. I gave a little cough, which kind of led to a gag. I was nearly sick. Oliver's mum was looking at me with that same confused look her son had so clearly inherited from her. My hand was still in my pocket. I dug deep as if I hadn't found it yet, as if I had many things in there, and not the one thing I'd obsessed over. I pulled out my love affair, that red-check hat that was beginning to lose Oliver's scent and had started picking up too many of Saada's hairs. I turned to Rupert, quick thinking, and said:

"Oliver, is it? I read your name on the label, my grandfather was called Oliver." He wasn't, Aiden. His name was Harry, but that's not the point. I needed to seem more human. Rupert just squinted at me, his glasses back at his side. His mother smiled, warmly. She'd bought my act. She poked her head back inside the house.

"Oliver! Oliver get down here!" She turned back to me. "That really is very kind of you, that's Rupert though." She nodded towards Rupert.

"Our eldest son is Oliver."

"Oh," I replied, as if this were news to me.

"Where is that boy? Excuse me, I'll just go and get him for you. He absolutely loves that hat. I'm sure he'll want to thank you himself." *So, the east London accent must have come from his father's side of the family.*

"Oh, don't worry I really should..." I started to panic. I wasn't ready to meet Oliver, not yet. Not after everything I'd dreamt about. I wasn't ready to push those dreams off of clouds and see if they would plummet or fly.

"He's just coming, look." Oliver's mother stepped aside, and a particularly tired looking Oliver came to the door with little bits of sleep caught in his long eyelashes. He rubbed his eyes and looked up at me. His uniform had practically been thrown onto him.

"Oliver, this is Ms..." She waved a hand, palm up, in my direction, pouted her lips and squinted her eyes. I panicked again, looking around for inspiration. Images of the police jumping into my head again, my face appearing on the area's most wanted list. I don't think we have one, but I'm pretty sure I'd be on it by now if we did.

"Ms. Bridges," I caved. I couldn't think of another suitable surname, looking around the only other options were: Ms. Terrace, Ms. Green or Ms. Vauxhall. None of those would do. I am not a character from *Cluedo.*

"Well, Oliver, Ms. Bridges has been so kind as to bring your hat back for you." Oliver's eyes trailed from his mother's to my hands, and a faint smile appeared on his face. His eyes ran up my body, and everything I owned was on fire. His eyes met mine, his head cocked to one side, recognition covered his face. I saw it. His mother saw it. His mother looked back to me, a questioning look on her face. I felt my face turn white hot.

"Thanks," Oliver whispered, his eyes dancing between each of mine. For a while, we all stood there, like cats in the street. Thank God for Rupert and his stubbed toe.

"Mum, Mum? I think I might need to go to hospital. I'm not joking Mum, the nail's coming off and everything."

Everyone moved at once. I held the hat out over the garden hedge. Oliver's mother ran back into the house shouting for Oliver's father, Jeffrey. Rupert began muttering to himself, cursing his inability to wear contacts. Oliver started towards me, his eyes trained on mine. I leant forward a little, over the hedge, and smiled my most human smile. Saada was pulling at my side wanting to move on, and I gave a gentle but firm tug back. Oliver noticed. He reached out for the hat. I reached in to try and make his life easier. We both leant towards each other, too fast, our knuckles clashed over the hedge.

"Sorry," I mumbled. He took the hat from my grasp, his fingertips brushing the backs of my hand. They are so soft Aiden, oh so soft.

"Thanks," he whispered again, testing a smile at me. I probably held onto the hat for a second too long. It was my armour, my excuse to be here. I could hardly come back with a football boot that I also accidently stumbled upon.

"I thought I lost it months ago..." The recognition clicked in his eyes. His chin raised a touch as if he finally remembered where he'd seen me. His mouth grew taut.

"Well...good things come to those who wait." *Good things come to those who wait? Good things come to those who bloody wait? What was that?* I actually said that to him, like I am some kind of lost prophet. I cringed before I even finished the sentence and shrunk into my coat as much as possible. I kind of expected him to put the hat on, but he didn't. He just stood there holding it, looking at me.

"Oliver? Oliver Harp, we're off. Thank Ms. Bridges for returning your hat; she didn't have to do that. We'll see you at six. Don't forget to put the oven on for me." Oliver's mother turned to Jeffrey and Rupert. "Come on boys, we're late enough as it is." She was rushing across the garden towards us.

I took a step back from the hedge. She grabbed Oliver's head and kissed it. Oliver squirmed out of her grip with his eyes still on mine.

"Have a nice day, Mister," she whispered into his hair. Oliver waved a dismissive arm like he was batting away a nuisance fly.

"It was lovely to meet you, Ms. Bridges. It's nice to know that there are still a few Good Samaritans out there."

I smiled.

With that, Oliver's father, mother, and a hobbling Rupert swept down the lane, into the car and drove off. Oliver and I stood in silence for a few minutes watching the events pan out in front of us.

"What's your mother's name?"

"Audrey." *Beautiful.*

"Oh." I nodded and began counting the last few daisies that had survived the winter. I felt like a giant looking down on a cluster of mountain peaks. I felt cumbersome and out of place.

"I better get to school."

"What about your friends?" I turned to the green expecting to see Samuel and the other boy waiting for him, watching us. Thank God I did turn because at the silence that followed, I realised what I'd said and could not help but let the mistake show on my face. How could Mummy be so stupid, Honey? I was so careless with my words. I composed myself and slowly turned back to Oliver. He was squinting at me, curious. He said nothing, as we both realised that I'd said too much.

"They're not coming today. They've gone on a school trip to Stoke-on-Trent. Mum and Dad said it wasn't worth the money." He spoke slowly now, double-checking every word he said, being careful as to what information he was giving away to this overly kind stranger. Saada pulled on her lead again. He'd taken a step back from the hedge since I'd turned around to the green. I was losing him.

"Bye, Ms. Bridges, it was nice to meet you, and thanks again for the hat." It was more of a dismissal than a mutual goodbye.

No, no, no, no. I couldn't leave it like this. Not after everything I'd dreamt, not after everything I'd imagined since that day our worlds had narrowly avoided colliding outside the tobacco store. I started walking, slowly, in the direction of his school. I heard the creak of his garden fence behind me followed by gentle, cautious footsteps echoing mine. I let Saada off her lead and prayed that she'd do something that would cause me to stop. In true Saada style, she decided to deposit her waste, right there, right then, a few steps in front of Oliver. I'd never been so happy to clean up her mess. I pulled a cellophane bag out of my pocket and with a suppressed smile on my face, knelt down to pick up yesterday's dinner. Oliver's footsteps slowed, I kept my back to him. They stopped, and I looked up. Our eyes met again, across a pile of poo. It was sublime.

"Who'd have thought something so gross could come out of something so nice?"

I laughed at Oliver's comment. It was true. We both looked at Saada with her wagging tail and her wonky smile creasing her dark eyes. I thanked every God there is and was for sending her in my direction. The atmosphere between us was lifted by your angels.

"Saada, meet Oliver. Oliver, Saada."

A genuine smile flooded his face revealing his pristine white teeth—all except one on the bottom row, which was an off-yellow. I overlooked the imperfection. It is the imperfections that make us perfect. Oliver knelt down to say hello and received a friendly lick on the chin. I couldn't lose him now, Aiden. I decided to play my trump card.

"Do you want to walk her with me?" Oliver stood up abruptly, snapped out of Saada's trance. I persisted.

"I'm walking her past school." I thought I'd revealed too much again so continued quickly. "I'm guessing you go to John Bramston?" Oliver nodded. Saada nuzzled his leg, and he smiled down at her again, his hesitance melting away. He shrugged his shoulders.

"Why not?"

5th May

Dear Aiden,

I walk past Oliver's house at 8:05 every morning. For a while, his friends walked with us. Then, for a while, they trailed a few steps behind us. In the end, they just stopped waiting on the green altogether. It is perfect. I'll exchange a few words about the weekend or the weather with Jeffrey and Audrey over the garden gate. Oliver rushes out the front door, sees that we've noticed his haste and slouches back into a nonchalant stroll. He'll give his parents that adorable dismissive wave as they sneak a kiss on his head when he passes. He'll always greet Saada before me. Kneeling, getting her worked up for the rest of her journey. But I don't mind that. He'll turn to me after.

"Morning, Ms. Bridges."

"Good morning, Oliver. All set to go?"

We'll wave off his parents and Rupert before beginning our journey down Arweneck Avenue. Both of us will become engrossed with whatever Saada is engrossed in, stopping to see what she's found, laughing at the treasures she brings back to us. I'll always leave him on the corner of the road his school is on. I don't want to embarrass him in front of his friends, and I don't want people to talk. Believe me, Honey, people around here can talk. We've flown over too many garden fences, as it is, you and I.

Oliver and I have been walking with each other for about two months now, and things have settled into routine quite nicely. We'll chat about silly little things that have happened at home, tiffs he's had with his brother, the same sort I imagine you and your siblings will have one day, Aiden. I've introduced him to a game I've been desperate to teach you. It's called And Then. I used to play it with your aunty Fi when I was Oliver's age.

I'll always start. I'll start with something mundane. Something like: "Barbara and Oliver were walking to school, and then..." It always takes Oliver a while to get into the swing of things. We'll test each other's imaginations while constantly having to remain straight faced. We'll push each other that little bit further until one of us finally caves, and we'll both fall into fits of laughter.

The game is marvellous, Aiden. Oliver and I will play the whole way to school or reminisce over past stories we've invented. We'll create private little worlds on every stroll and make subtle references to them in front of Oliver's parents. Of course, they'll never catch on and it gives Oliver and I something to smirk about later. It brings us closer together.

Dear Aiden,

Today, I've decided to make Oliver a sandwich for him to take to school. He's mentioned a few times that the prices for school lunches are going up, but he doesn't have the heart to tell his mother that he needs more lunch money. Instead, he'll skip lunches some days so he can eat properly with his friends another day. He doesn't seem to mind so much about skipping a lunch, but that's no way to bring up a child. No. We'll raise him properly, or at least as best we can.

What do 12-year-old boys have in their sandwiches? I scanned the cupboards. I have canned tuna, peanut butter, marmite, some pineapple rings, herbs and maple syrup. What if he has a nut allergy? What if he's glucose, lactose, or dairy intolerant, as half the world seems to be these days? I headed to the fridge. There must be a safer bet. There's ham, salmon, and cream cheese. A jar of raspberry jam sits at the back of the fridge. You can never go wrong with a jam sandwich. I decided to slice off two ends of crusts and left the other two on. Crusts make your hair grow curly, you know? I think Oliver's hair is probably curly enough as it is. By the time I'm finished wrapping the sandwich in tin foil and writing his name on the top, it's 7:45. I popped a jelly cube in my mouth, grabbed Saada and headed out the door.

Oliver bounded out of the front door at exactly 8:05. I was just walking up the street, and to my delight a look of panic crossed his face when he thought I wasn't there. Saada barked her greeting, and Oliver looked our way and beamed. My belly warmed at the sight. *It feels so good to be wanted. Now, we just need to be needed.* He turned back and called a goodbye to his family.

"Hang on a second, Love!" Audrey rushed out the front door, pulling a cardigan on over her blouse and looking beautiful as ever. I held Saada back, my smile wavering a little.

"Come here." Oliver looked at me and back to his mother. *Torn?* He headed back towards her. She held his head and kissed his forehead. I averted my gaze.

"Have a good day, Handsome." Oliver tried to squirm out of his mother's grip, but she held onto him. "Morning, Ms. Bridges." She smiled over to me, and I felt my face flush red. "I hope he's being on his best behaviour with you during these walks?"

"Mum, come on!" Oliver rolled his eyes and slapped his hand to his face.

"What?" She looked at her son, playing the innocent.

"You're embarrassing me," he mumbled. She smiled, a wicked smile.

Mission accomplished then.

She looked back to me and gave his hair a vigorous rub, sending curls flying out of place.

"You know, if Saada ever does her business on these walks, Oliver is always more than happy to pick it up for you. We need to make the most of those young knees." I laughed, and Oliver groaned as he was finally released from his mother's embrace. He ran out of the front garden and bent down to greet Saada.

"I'll keep that in mind. Thanks, Audrey."

Oliver stood up and slipped the lead out of my hand before I got a chance to object. Our hands touched for a moment, and I was reminded of how soft his skin is. I got the overwhelming urge to ruffle his curls just as Audrey had, but I refrained and slipped my hands into my pockets instead. We headed off down the street.

"You're not really going to make me pick up Saada's poop are you, Ms. Bridges?"

"I wouldn't dream of it." He looked up at me with that same beaming smile that I can see so many girls will fall in love with one day.

There was no game of And Then today. I don't know why I felt so nervous about giving him a sandwich. It's a sandwich for crying out loud, who doesn't want a free sandwich? Clearly my mind was on other things. Thankfully, Oliver was too consumed with Saada to notice. The innocence of youth is a beautiful thing. We turned onto the road that connected us to the road of his school, and I stopped walking. Oliver and Saada carried on at least 10 metres before realising. He turned around to face me.

"Everything okay, Ms. Bridges?" He cocked his head to one side, and my heart melted a little.

"I just. I just wanted to give you something before we say goodbye." This got his attention. He gave Saada a gentle tug, and the two headed back to me.

"What is it?"

"Well, first of all, it's a secret. So, you can't tell anyone that I gave it to you, okay?" I didn't need any of his friends at school blabbing that it was unfair because Oliver was getting two lunches: one from his mum and the other from the crazy lady with the dog. Plus, I certainly didn't need him telling his brother or Audrey hearing about how I am feeding her son. The last thing any mother needs is another woman stepping into her role because she's not doing it well enough. I can tell she cares, there's just always room for improvement.

"Okay," he replied, tilting his head a little more.

"I'm serious, Oliver, you can't tell anyone." He dropped Saada's lead to the ground, but she wasn't going anywhere anyway.

"Cross my heart and hope to die." He crossed his heart with one hand while holding the other, palm flat in the air, like a Brownie promise.

That felt a good enough promise as any. I pulled the slightly crumpled jam sandwich from my pocket and presented it, like a sacrifice to the Gods. I may as well have been on my knees offering it to him.

"A sandwich?" He burst out laughing. It wasn't the reaction I imagined. "That's the big secret? A sandwich?" He was shaking his head laughing. I smiled, feeling a little embarrassed at how seriously I'd taken this whole event. Still, he didn't take it from my hands. I decided to play along with him.

"I'm serious, Oliver. *No one* can know about this jam sandwich, okay?" I said, smiling at him. He took it, shaking his head in disbelief.

"You had me for a minute there, Ms. Bridges." He slipped his rucksack off his back and put the sandwich inside. "But, thank you." He smiled at me as he swung his rucksack back on. "I'm sure it will be the best jam sandwich I've ever had." I winked at him and picked up Saada's lead.

We continued along the road a little further before we said our brief goodbyes in front of passing parents. I always made a show of acting like our goodbye was nothing. That our relationship was innocent and had occurred because we were just family friends walking in the same direction. Yet, every time we say goodbye, my heart drops a little. It feels so good to be wanted, but to be needed is something else entirely. I wasn't needed yet.

20th June

Dear Aiden,

Spring has quickly rolled into summer, and my walks with Oliver have been consistent. They've been the highlight of every day. What was once a secret sandwich turned into a sandwich and a chocolate bar, which then turned into the previous two with some fruit and a carton of juice. The days grew into weeks, and I now send Oliver off to school with a lunch box. Some days, I'll leave notes in there for him. Nothing too much, just in case it falls into the wrong hands. I'll wish him luck if he has a spelling test or a sports competition—things I don't even think Audrey knows about, which is nothing against her, since Rupert can be a lot to handle at times. More often than not, Oliver is pushed to the side for his kid brother. He's pushed to the side and out of the nest before he's ready to fly. But it's okay; he's landed in my nest now. I'll look after him.

Today is his last day of school before he breaks up for the summer holidays. I'd got so lost in our perfect routine that I'd forgotten how easily it could be broken. Today, I'll need to play a different game, and I'll need to play it very carefully.

I was waiting outside Oliver's a little earlier than usual. Audrey must have spotted me through the window because she came rushing out.

"Morning, Barbara, are you here earlier today or are we running late?"

I smiled warmly back at her. "Don't worry, I'm here early." She had already begun heading back inside.

"Well, I'll see if Oliver is ready, but you know better than I do what he's like."

Damn right.

"Actually, Audrey, I came early because it was you I wanted to speak to. Do you have a minute?" She looked back at me, this had never happened before. She brushed her hands off on her jeans, sensing something sober in the air and headed towards me, arms crossed.

"What's up? Is everything okay?"

"Everything is fine, don't worry."

"Oh, God. He's upset you, hasn't he? What's he done? I could kill that boy." I winced. If only we could all have the luxury.

"No, not at all. Don't be silly. I actually wanted to ask you a favour." This is where I needed to tread carefully. I needed to ensure that not one hint of crazy was passed over this garden gate.

"Of course, anything." She smiled at me, and her shoulders dropped an inch.

"Well, you know it's Oliver's last day of school today, before summer." Her mouth dropped open.

"You're kidding me, right? How did I not even realise this? Rupert doesn't break up for another week!"

There's your answer, Sweetie.

She turned to head inside, but I grabbed her arm, perhaps a little too hard. She swung back towards me and looked down at my hand, gripping her.

"Sorry," I whispered. I let go of her arm.

"What's wrong, Love? Wait, does he have a half day today? Crap, I'll need to leave work early. No one's going to be free at such short notice. A couple of hours and he's okay, but I can't leave him alone for so long." She started talking more to herself than to me. She pulled out her mobile. It was now or never to make my move.

"Audrey," I whispered. I had her full attention at the tone of my voice; the mobile was back in her pocket. "I'm sure you must have heard about me? About what happened to me and my son?"

She looked guilty, incredibly guilty. Her eyes jumped to the bush.

"I did overhear a few of the mums at parent's evening..." This is not something I needed to know and we both knew it. "I wasn't sure how much of it was true and what was just hearsay." She looked me in the eyes again.

"What you've heard is probably true, or close to it."

She nodded, and I continued before she could interject, while I still had control over my actions. "I lost my son, Aiden, last summer. He was born still. I held him until his body turned cold in my arms." I could feel tears pricking at the corner of my eyes, and I looked to the sky.

Keep it together, Barbara.

"I had such big plans for us, Audrey. He was going to be a musician. He was going to go to med school. He had a heart of pure gold."

Stop, Barbara, stop.

I shook my head and brought my eyes back to hers. "I've had a rough few months, Audrey. I'm being completely honest in saying that your son has helped me through more than he knows. Our walks with Saada, well, they give me something to get up for in the mornings. I know this is an odd request, but I was wondering if you'd let him keep walking with me throughout the summer? If he wants to, of course." I smiled through watery eyes, realising how much truth I was finally speaking. "I just don't know what I'll do if I have no one to get out of bed for."

Audrey flung her arms around me and held me to her, over the garden gate. Her tears were streaming down the side of my face, and I eventually hugged her back.

"Of course, Barbara. Oh God, of course."

"Eew! What are you two doing?" Oliver's voice chimed behind us. Audrey cried a little harder while her shoulders jerked up and down. "Mum?" We broke apart, and Audrey smiled at me through teary eyes, nodding her approval over and over again.

She turned to Oliver. "Are you ready for your last day of school, Dear?"

He looked at her, and his eyes narrowed.

"Yes."

"Good. Mummy has to work like normal today." She turned to me. "But maybe you could ask Ms. Bridges if she'd want to walk you home?"

I looked at her, shaking my head in disbelief. How can someone so beautiful be so kind? Oliver walked up to us and beamed up at me.

"That'd be cool. Do you think you could, Ms. Bridges?" He put his hands under his chin framing his face and blinking up at me through those long lashes.

"Of course." I wasn't even going to attempt to play hard to get, I couldn't stop smiling and shaking my head.

"Perfect," Audrey said as she went to mess up Oliver's hair, but he ducked out of her way and hopped the garden gate. "You're finishing at lunch then, Oli?"

"Yup."

"So, if you could be outside the school gates at one, that would be great, Ms. Bridges?" She acted as if I was doing her a favour.

Such kindness.

"Consider me there." Oliver reached down to greet Saada and began telling her how lucky she was to be seeing him twice in the same day. Audrey leaned a little closer towards me.

"I'll leave it with you to talk to him about the summer holidays," she whispered.

"Thanks." I turned to Oliver and Saada. "Shall we?"

"We shall," he replied.

"Have a nice day, Love." Audrey called before rushing back inside.

I decided to dive straight in. "Oliver, I know today is your last day of school before the summer holidays, so as of next week you won't need to wake up so early. But I was wondering if you'd still want to walk Saada with me in the mornings?"

"Are you kidding me?" My heart dropped a moment. "Of course, I'll still walk Saada with you. I can't wait to actually go on a walk for longer than 15 minutes. I want to take Saada over the forest. Have you been?"

Panic over.

"There's only one thing though," he said.

Panic restarted. Oliver continued. "You have to bring a lunch sometimes. I need my jam sandwiches." He laughed, and I laughed with him. It was almost a triumphant laugh.

He needed me, Aiden. This boy finally needed me. Albeit for jam sandwiches, but still, the premise was there. We reached the school gates. I'd never walked this far with him before but thought nothing of it now that I had Audrey's approval. There was spring in our steps and summer on the way. The quicker we got Oliver into school, the quicker he would be out, and we would all be reunited again...one big happy family.

"I'll see you after school then, Love." I couldn't help but say it, and it felt so great to say. I don't care who heard.

"See you, Ms. Bridges!"

We'll work on that response. I practically bounced all the way home, planning our afternoon together the whole way.

Dear Aiden,

I was outside the gates at 12:40. There was no way I was going to be late. Not today, not ever. Other mums started to gather around me, flocking together like birds at breadcrumbs. I stood patiently with Saada at my side for 20 minutes.

The school bell rang throughout the playground and I couldn't help but break into a smile, my chin held high, my hair brushed out of my face. I stood, proudly waiting for my boy. I scanned the faces bobbing across the playground, children cutting across each other like London traffic, each one eager to get home. I saw mums and dads waving enthusiastically at their children and those same children shrinking into their uniform. Some were literally face palming themselves out of embarrassment.

One mother, who I'm 99 percent sure had whispered your name just minutes before, greeted her son with open arms. He threw his lunch box at her and exclaimed, "Where's the car?"

The mother caught the lunch box and looked around, hoping no one had heard. I made sure she caught eye contact with me. *I'd heard.* At that exact moment, Oliver came bounding up to me, all smiles and joy.

"Hi, Love. Happy holidays!" I squealed, sharing his excitement. He grinned back at me and threw his fists in the air.

"Freedom!" he cried. We both laughed together, and I looked back at the lunch-box-catching mother to my left. She scoffed at me, spun on her heels and went in search of her son and the car.

Karma is as sweet as a Jam sandwich.

We continued away from the school entrance and circled the school grounds before heading back to Oliver's home. When we got to his front gate I stopped, and Oliver continued talking as he headed towards the front door and began fumbling for his keys. He realised I hadn't crossed the gate when he was slipping off his other shoe in the porch.

"Aren't you coming in, Ms. Bridges?" I'd never crossed the garden gate before.

"I don't know. I've got Saada with me. I don't want her hair getting everywhere." He thought for a moment.

"Let's put Saada in the back garden, I want to show you something." I couldn't exactly argue with that, could I? He closed the front door, and I considered bolting down the street with Saada at my side and telling him something came up. A family issue, no questions asked. I was just about to turn away when the side gate swung open. Oliver beckoned us over and in we went. My shoulders were tense, and I felt like I'd forgotten how to walk. I adopted an awkward gait that didn't feel right and I could only imagine how much worse it must have looked. We headed around the side of the house and reached a back garden that was everything I expected it to be. Potted plants dotted the edge of a small piece of decking at the back of the garden. The decking was adorned with a table and chairs for four. A minia-ture football goal was sitting in the other corner of the garden and an assortment of balls was lying at rest around it. There was a pair of patio doors swinging on their hinges and Oliver went back to pin them open. He turned to Saada, whose tail was wagging at a rate I'd never witnessed before.

"Now Saada, you're not allowed in the house. Not yet anyway. So, stay." He put a finger to her nose and I dropped the lead. We headed inside. The dining room ran the entire way across the bottom floor. Light flooded in from both ends and I looked out at the garden gate that I stood at for so many mornings past. I saw myself there now and how sad I must look, waiting for a 12-year-old boy to come out and play.

To my disappointment, there were no fairy lights above the dining room table. Yet, nothing could have prepared me for the smell of the place. The smell sent me back to Nana's place when I was a child. It was a mix of natural soap, garlic and this warming family smell that no one has ever been able to define.

Oliver led me through the dining room to the stairs and up we went. I felt guilty, like I was taking advantage of a child left home alone. But then, what was there to take advantage of? I suppose we've become friends over the last few months. Granted it's an odd pairing and perhaps frowned upon by some, but there was nothing malicious behind it. Oliver needed me, and I needed Oliver. We were helping each other. I kept my eyes to the floor. I felt like I was invading his family's private space.

At the top of the stairs, we turned left and left again, and he threw open the door to his bedroom. A single bed was in the far right corner next to the window that overlooked Arweneck Avenue. The bottom half of the walls was covered in a dark blue wallpaper, the top half in a light cream, with images of planets separating the two colours. There were glow-in-the-dark stars above his bed and a games console on a desk with a small TV on the wall in front of it. He took a few steps, turned to me and raised his arm to the left.

"*This* is what I wanted to show you." The right-hand-side of his wall was filled with shelves, which were covered in hundreds of various Lego creations, from the tiniest of wizards to the greatest of boats and planes. He looked at me with pure pride covering his face. He crossed his arms and stood, nodding his approval at his own collection.

"Wow, Oliver. This is, incredible! How many things do you have here?"

"I know, I know. I have 257 pieces in total. Mum says I'm too old for it now, but some Lego actually starts at 16 and up. Besides, the maximum age is 99, which is centuries away, so I don't think I have anything to worry about. Look." He headed over to a chest of plastic drawers under the shelves; they were translucent, and I could see they were stacked with magazines. He pulled out the top one. It was a Lego magazine.

"This is what I'm saving for."

The magazine fell open on a page that had clearly been opened more than the rest. He placed his index finger with such affirmation on the page that I thought he'd punch through it. It was a New York-style firefighter's house. It had 4,634 pieces and was aged 16+. It came with the full cast from *Ghostbusters.* This kid meant business.

Oliver began reeling off every bit of information he knew about the firefighter's house. He put the book on the floor and I knelt alongside him. His hands flew through the air as he described how big the finished piece would be. I heard nothing. I just looked at him and tried to take in as much of his face as possible, so I could replay it before I fall asleep at night. My dreams are a sweeter, safer place with Oliver in them.

After he was done talking about the firefighter's house, he started flicking through the magazine to show me other things he had his eye on. Occasionally he'd get up and pull down one of his models from the shelf, explaining their similarity but why it was important that he had both. Clearly, he'd had to go through this argument a few times in the past. I imagined his father sighing and exclaiming: "Come on, Oli. You've already got three Lego helicopters. How can this one be any different?"

I eventually shuffled back on the carpet and rested my back against the wall with my legs out in front of me. Oliver began taking me through each of his pieces. If they had functional parts, I witnessed how it worked and he took it apart and showed me why it worked the way it did. Their structure fascinated him, and I saw glimpses of him 20 years down the line. Perhaps he'd be an engineer? A mechanic?

I don't know how long we were in Oliver's room, but his ears pricked up to something I was clearly not accustomed to listening for.

"Mum's home. Don't tell her I've been showing you my Lego collection all this time, okay?"

"Oli!? Oliver, what have I told you about leaving your shoes by the front door!" He blushed red and rushed out of his room to the top of the stairs.

"Ms. Bridges is here, Mum," he called down the stairs, and I could hear the strain in his voice as he urged his mum not to tell him off in front of company.

"Oh...hi, Barbara!" she called up the stairs, clearly a little taken aback. Like a sheepish girlfriend, I came out of Oliver's room.

"Hi, Audrey." I joined Oliver at the top of the stairs. She stood at the bottom of the stairs twirling her keys in her hands, one shoe off.

"Um, would you like to stay for tea? It's Friday, takeout night!" Oliver threw his fists up in the air again. He's had quite a triumphant day so far. Audrey smiled, relaxing a little and I started heading down the stairs.

"Thank you for the offer, Audrey, but I should actually get going. I think we lost track of time up there, and Saada is still out in the back garden." Oliver groaned from behind me. I think it's been a while since anyone has shown interest in his Lego collection.

"Saada can have my leftovers," he tried from the top of the stairs. We all smiled.

"What have you two been up to then?" Audrey tried to remain as casual as possible, but there was just the slightest defensive tone to her voice. Maybe her son hadn't noticed, but I had.

Oliver jumped in. "We, umm, well, we've been up here starting on my summer project. Haven't we, Ms. Bridges?" His voice cracked a tone higher, and I was sure we'd see sweat prickling across his brow if had he be down there with us. Audrey raised an eyebrow.

"We certainly have. He's got blocks and blocks of it for the summer, all stacked away up there." The penny dropped for Audrey. Oliver, not quite so much.

"Exactly!" he exclaimed. "See you tomorrow, Ms. Bridges." He quit while he was ahead and rushed back into his room.

The door quickly closed, and I imagined him returning each Lego creation to its designated place before his mother managed to come up the stairs. She turned to me.

"Sorry you had to go through that. I've told him a hundred times, he's too old for Legos."

I laughed. "Absolutely no need to apologise. I actually guiltily enjoyed it. His passion for building is pretty mesmerizing."

"Trust me, the novelty soon wears off when you're finding Lego pieces in places you didn't know existed." I laughed with Audrey. "We have a little league match tomorrow. You're more than welcome to join us. It's on Hainault Common, and the game starts at nine. We put a little whisky in our coffee to help get us through the morning."

"Sounds good. I'll see what I can do. Audrey, thank you for what you're doing. I really appreciate it."

"Please, don't ever thank me again, Barbara. Seriously, I can't even imagine..." She trailed off, and I dropped my head.

"Maybe see you tomorrow," I mumbled into my chest.

She put a hand on my shoulder. "I genuinely hope so, Barbara."

I headed out the backdoor. Saada had fallen asleep in the last patch of sun in the corner of the garden on the decking.

"Let's get out of here, Saada." I called. She shook off the dirt and sleep from her coat and bounded over to me. "Sorry for leaving you so long, Love." Me and Saada. Saada, I, and a little Lego wizard in my pocket, united against the world.

21st June

Dear Aiden,

Oliver's match went well this morning. His team won 3–2. Oliver, of course, scored two of those goals. *That's my boy.* He kept yelling across the pitch, "Did you see that, Ms. Bridges? Did you see that tackle?" At first, I was a little worried at how the other parents would react. I quickly struck a joke that I was his new favourite because I was the only one willing to put up with his Lego stories. The mood quickly relaxed among the parents around me, and every time he called out to me after that we all chuckled. It was *glorious.*

We drank mugs of steaming hot coffee with hits of whisky. I felt like this was the secret life of parents—just kids pretending to be grown-ups. We gossip, we bitch, we booze, and say things like, "Do as we say, not as we do." Of course, Saada barked her approval alongside the pitch for the first half of the game. Rupert kept her entertained for the second half, giving all of us a break. During halftime, the mums whipped out cartons of juice and sliced oranges. We all sat on the sidelines talking tactics alongside their coach. For some reason, we all thought we had the best advice for the team. I couldn't help but get involved. Every time I fell quiet, Oliver would look over at me, smile, and draw me back into the heat of the team pep talk.

This must be what it's like, Aiden. This is the dream that so many are living but no one is realising. A world full of mums and dads, grandmothers and grandfathers. They're all finding so much happiness in the everyday tasks of parenthood. These people don't know how lucky they are. For them, everything worked out; it probably didn't even cross their minds when their kids were just bumps. I suppose they slipped into parenthood as easily as they slip into their pyjamas at night.

During some of the nastier tackles in the football game, I winced. These lives are so fragile, and we only have one on this Earth. The parents would give a pantomime boo or hiss as a child would roll around on the floor clutching his knee. It happened to Oliver once and I yelped and went to run on the pitch. Jeffrey called me back.

"Barbara," he said. "Relax, it's all part of the show, just watch."

Oliver continued to roll around on the floor screaming in agony until the referee ran up to him and the culprit that had done the damage.

"Ref! Ref!" Jeffrey was yelling from behind me, echoed by the other parents. The ref looked down at Oliver, and then looked at the other boy that had taken him to the floor. He pulled a yellow card from his back pocket and thrust it into the air. The parents around me howled their approval like a pack of wolves and burst out laughing. They turned and high-fived each other and their success. Oliver hopped into the air and skipped off back to his position, mission complete. I grinned at the charade. *So, it's that kind of game, is it?* Clearly the whisky was starting to kick in.

After the game, Oliver came bounding up to us. His team-mates followed closely behind, found their parents in the crowd, and were received with triumphant yelps. To my disappointment, Oliver didn't come running to me first, and I took it as a slap around the face. Silly me. Of course, he's not going to come to Mummy Barbara first. We just have to be patient and eventually he will.

The team, and its company, started to disperse once we reached the car park. Tipsy farewells were called over car rooftops as one sober parent ushered the whiskey-fuelled other into the passenger seat. I stood on the grass verge chatting away with Jeffrey when a flushed Audrey approached us with the boys in tow.

"Barbara, the boys have something they would like to ask you," she giggled and pushed both of them forward. Rupert elbowed Oliver in his side. Oliver cleared his throat.

"The Harps are having a start of summer barbecue this afternoon, and Rupert wants to know if you would come?"

"Hey!" Rupert called out. "That's not fair! It isn't just me, Oliver wants it too!" Rupert stuck out his bottom lip and looked as if he was about to cry, his glasses slipping off his button nose more so than usual as he began shaking his head.

Audrey laughed again. "Unfortunately, this would be an invite only to you, Barbara. My brother is coming, and his kids are both allergic to dogs." She rolled her eyes as if she couldn't possibly believe what she was saying.

"What time?" I asked, before they had a chance to change their mind. Audrey looked taken aback for a moment before smiling.

"We're lighting the barbecue at four. You're welcome anytime around then."

"Need me to bring anything?" I needed to keep this conversation strictly business. I didn't trust myself to do much more.

"If you can get your hands on a good vino, it will definitely be appreciated," she grinned. She may as well have hiccupped.

"I'll see what I can do." I smiled back at her, feeling the warmth of the whisky in my gut. I continued to nod as I turned away from the family. My brow furrowed. I should have a few bottles in storage from mine and Aunty Fi's trip to France a few years back.

"We could do with some time apart, couldn't we, Saada? It'll be good for us both." She panted up at me and that was the extent of our conversation.

Pleased you agree.

I got home and immediately jumped in the shower, I needed to wash away the whisky and be as fresh-faced as possible for this barbecue. I can't imagine the other parents putting as much thought into it, but no doubt they'd been to these events before. These were family events. You have to have more than a dog to get invited to these sorts of events.

Once I was out of the shower, I started sifting through my wardrobe to find suitable, *mumsy* attire. I needed to look the part, after all. I pulled out Rupert's football boot and threw it into the front room alongside your gifts. I couldn't deal with Rupert right now. The little Lego wizard watched over everything from my bedside table, my guardian angel. I finally found a beige pair of chinos and an oversized, peach shirt. I threw it on and went to look at myself in the full-length mirror. My hair needed work. My eyes were alive, though. They shone hues I never knew existed, catching greens and blues and striping them with yellow. I was getting there. I was starting to glow again. I began to work on my hair. It needed to look casually great; no one could know that I tried too hard. I ran two small plaits through it and then tied it all back. It took a few attempts to get them how I wanted them. That was the trickiest part, making it look suitably scruffy but not messy. I finally found a casual balance between practical and pretty—exactly what I wanted. I put a touch of blusher on and did my eyes. I didn't want to overdo it with the makeup. I brushed my teeth for the third time, and then I accepted that the whisky was coming through my pores, and it wasn't going to get much better than that. I took a breath and looked in the mirror once more.

The sun has brought out some of my freckles; they dot my skin like the first, brave stars at night. My cheeks were still rosy from the morning's activities. Mummy scrubs up well when she wants to. I think I looked the part. I painted my nails and walked around the house flaring my fingers and toes for 10 minutes until it all dried. I found a pair of white sandals and slipped them on. The look was complete. I was complete in just over an hour and the barbecue didn't start for three more.

I got the wine I wanted out of the rack and put it in the fridge. Saada was sanctioned to the garden. I couldn't go covered in dog hair. The last thing I needed was to be told to leave because I'd started some poor child's allergic reaction. I slid onto a kitchen chair and sat, embracing the quiet for all of five minutes. I couldn't do it for any longer; I was too agitated. I got up. What needed to be done around the house? What could I do that wouldn't require too much? I looked around the kitchen once more and then realised what was ticking away at me. Everything was still childproofed. The cabinets still had those white child locks on them and the corners of the display cabinet were still covered in polystyrene. How have I gone all these months without realising this? It's not that we won't use them again one day, Love, but for now I'm going to take them down. I'll put them away somewhere safe, for the future. For *our* future.

I arrived at the barbecue a little past four. The locks had proven trickier to remove than I expected. I chipped some of my nail polish but that was okay, it added to my look. I am a practical woman. The noise from the garden made it sound as though the barbecue was already in full swing. I could hear music from the front of the house. I suppose a few parents had gone directly from the game. However, as I followed the sign to head around the side of the house, another couple turned into the front garden behind me. I glanced over my shoulder and recognised the packed-lunch-catching mother from the school gates. I quickly turned back and scuttled through to the back garden.

Bunting had been strung up along the garden gate and over the entrance to the house, framing the patio doors in multi-coloured triangles. Oliver was practising shootouts with a group of boys and his little brother in one corner of the garden. The garden table had been pulled onto the grass and I recognised a few of the mums from the football match. The decking was covered with shirtless dads and their hairy guts, beers in hands, huffing and grunting over a ridiculously large barbecue. Jeffrey stood among them, the only one to remain with his shirt on; it was light pink with various fish on it. A pair of khaki shorts with too many pockets came to just below his knees. Although he stood at the centre of the barbecue with a set of tongs, he fell half a head shorter than the other men and they all seemed to talk over him. Jeffrey laughed when they did, and nodded his head when they did too, but he didn't say so much. He just stood there, flipping burgers that the other men would point at every now and again.

Audrey broke away from the gaggle of women that surrounded her. She was wearing a red one-piece swimming costume with a torn pair of denim shorts, her feet were bare, and her hair fell around her shoulders in waves. She looked incredible.

She headed towards a paddling pool filled with ice, different cans of beer, and bottles of various spirits. She snapped the lid off a beer and headed over to her husband. The men parted like the Red Sea, without saying a word as she passed. She kissed Jeffrey on the cheek and placed the beer bottle in his free hand, whispering something in his ear. His face flushed, and she strutted away. Every man's gaze followed her apart from Jeffrey's, who seemed more determined than ever to flip every burger on the barbecue. He took a long swig of his beer.

"I'll take a photo for you, Dave!" One of the mums called out "We can put it on the fridge next to our daughter's spelling test!" The mums cackled to one another and the men sheepishly closed their circle at the barbecue once more. Audrey threw a heel in the air and brushed her hair off her shoulder, to which the other mums cackled even louder. Audrey spotted me.

"Barbara! You brought wine!" she squealed and came tittering over to me. The other women watched, waiting for their moment to pass judgement. She took the wine out of my hands and gave me a brisk hug.

"I'll put it in the tub." She tittered away and placed the wine into the paddling pool before returning to her pack.

"Ms. Bridges?" I looked down to see a worried looking Rupert at my side. He tugged at my shirt and beckoned me to come down to his level. He cupped a hand around his mouth and whispered into my ear.

"Oliver told me he got to show you his Legos. I've got Legos, too. I'm not quite as good as Oli, but I've got loads of different ones. Do you want to play?"

"Sure, Honey." I was all too aware of drifting eyes wondering what this little boy was whispering into my ear. I stood to my full height again. "Just let me say hello to everyone first."

He skipped off towards his brother. "She said, YES!" The boys high-fived before turning back to the assortment of footballs that had been lined up alongside the other, ready to be pelted at a fierce looking girl standing in goal. The girl rolled up her sleeves and punched her chest. I hadn't noticed her before.

"Give me your best shot, Rupert!" She cried.

"One goal coming right up, Kelly!" Rupert shouted back. I smiled before turning towards the hyenas and their plastic cups of white wine or Pimms. A few of the mums noticed and kept their eyes trained on me.

"Barbara! Come and join us." Audrey waved me over. "Here." She poured me a glass of white wine and thrust it into my hand. "Barbara's been helping me with the boys over the past couple of months, she's been a lifesaver."

The irony.

I smiled at my appraisal and looked around the group. The other mums' features softened. One of them scooted over along the garden table and tapped the space next to her. I took my perch and tried to blend in as much as possible, sipping my wine.

So, this was how it felt to be a mum, Aiden. This is what we did in our spare time. We drank, we laughed, and we complained about our spouses.

"Tell me about it." One of the women rolled her eyes as we discussed the last topic.

"Hey! Don't you forget your other half is right here. I may be a foot shorter than you, but it doesn't affect my hearing." A woman with piercing blue eyes and brown shoulder length hair grabbed her partner around the back of the neck, wriggling her fingers into the sides, which set the taller of the two into a fit of giggles. Intense laughter caused her to swing her arms wildly knocking my glass out of my hand and sent the remainder of my wine down my shirt.

"Cassandra! Look what you've gone and done. Sorry Barbara, let's go and get you sorted out." She pushed her girlfriend's legs aside and stood up. "Audrey, do you have anything she can wear?"

Audrey got to her feet as well. "There's always one, isn't there, Cassandra?" she accused in mock anger. "Ladies, right this way."

The blue-eyed woman took my hand and Audrey took hers. I threw my bag over my shoulder. Just like that, we were the best of friends, off to fight the world. Or at least find Mummy a change of clothes. I wondered if Audrey's clothes would smell like Oliver's do.

I was led upstairs, hand still being held, and the door to Audrey's room was swung open. It was painted a faint lilac colour, it smelt of her perfume, and there was a grand French wardrobe in the centre of the back wall. Audrey opened both doors to the wardrobe and mirrors greeted me from the inside of each door. She started sifting through her wardrobe and throwing out various coloured playsuits that we both knew I'd look ridiculous in.

"Right, let's get you out of this." The blue-eyed woman approached me from behind and tried to tug my shirt off over my shoulders. I shrugged her off, probably a little too aggressively. She raised her hands to me.

"Hey, it's nothing we haven't seen before, I'm just trying to help," she said. I nodded my acknowledgement and swallowed hard, the taste of wine still on my lips. I walked over to the bed and Audrey waved her arms across everything.

"Take your pick, Love." I picked up a light blue blouse and walked to the corner of the room. With my back to them I slid my shirt off over my head. An awkward silence fell among them. I dropped my pink shirt to the floor, all too aware of the eyes on my back. Audrey came around the bed and picked it up off the floor.

"I'll throw this in the wash and get it back to you another day." She spoke so softly. I fumbled with the new blouse I'd been given, but I couldn't undo the buttons I was shaking so much.

"Let me." The blue-eyed woman came to my side and pulled the shirt out of my hands. I crossed my arms over my stomach while she stood alongside me and unbuttoned the blouse.

"Here." She offered the shirt back to me and I turned a little to take it from her.

"Thank you," I whispered. Her eyes caught mine and briefly flicked down my front. I know she spotted the scars across my stomach. A flicker of shock in her eyes, followed by sympathy, followed by normality once more. She was trying too hard, though. Her lips were pressed tight.

"Sorry for what happened to you with the wine. We were being stupid."

I threw the blouse around me and buttoned it up as quickly as I possibly could.

"No, it's fine. Honestly, don't worry about it."

"Okay, we'll head back downstairs. See you in a minute." The two quickly left the room and I can only imagine the looks they must have exchanged. Whereas before, they were so keen to help me, now they couldn't be quicker to leave me alone. Just like that, the three musketeers became one lonely mother and a scar-covered stomach.

I sat on the bed and took a few deeps breaths, rubbing my temples. I needed to bring this back; this was my big chance at becoming one of them. This would be good for us. I took one last deep breath and headed over to Audrey's vanity table, where I sifted through the perfumes until I found my favourite. I sprayed myself a couple of times, hoping that would be enough to mask the wine. I slipped the perfume into my bag and headed out the room. I almost walked directly into Rupert.

"Ms. Bridges! Can I please, please, please show you my Legos now?"

"Of course, Love." I wasn't quite ready to go back out yet anyway. Rupert took my hand and pushed open the door next to us.

"You smell like Mummy," he said idly, as he led me to his bed and sat me down. "You kind of look like her, too."

I blushed red, but Rupert was too preoccupied to notice.

Rupert's room must have been about half the size of his brother's. He had a small wardrobe squeezed in next to his single bed. At the bottom of his bed there was a white-framed bookshelf. I presume it was supposed to hold all of Rupert's things. But I could see that over the years, the family had slowly started putting miscellaneous valuables in there that had no other place in the home. The shelves were also flooded with crime fiction, and I'm pretty sure that isn't Rupert's first go-to genre. Along his windowsill lay a small array of Lego boats, cars and planes. The blocks were a little simpler than his big brothers'. I imagine the final product comes together a lot quicker than the 4,000-piece firefighter's house I saw the other day. Rupert began taking me through his various pieces in much the same way that his older brother had. No doubt Rupert had learned from him.

After 10 minutes or so, I heard women's voices floating around from outside Rupert's bedroom door. I wouldn't have paid attention to it normally, but there was something about the urgent tone of the voices that got my attention. I stood up and mocked a stretch, holding my back. I headed over to the door but stayed facing Rupert. He continued, not the least bit phased that his only audience member was floating around the auditorium. I'm pretty sure that even if I were not in the room, his speech would be exactly the same. He merely turned his body towards me and continued with his display. I turned my head slightly, but very obviously kept my eyes on Rupert.

"She probably went home."

"Can you blame her? I couldn't imagine the amount of pain coming to something like this would cause."

"But still, Louise, she was covered in scars. You should have seen how she reacted to me helping her. I wouldn't want that kind of aggression around my kids."

"Audrey is only trying to help, she's just doing her part."

I pushed my ear to the door. Rupert was next to me, a Lego submarine in his hand, and he pushed his ear to the door too.

"What are we listening for, Ms. Bridges?"

I pushed a finger to my lips.

"Mummy says it's rude to eavesdrop," he whispered. I turned my other ear to the door so that I was looking away from him. The women had stopped talking. I thought they'd heard us.

The chain flushed.

"I know Audrey is doing her part, but she needs to be careful. The woman lost her kid, and now she's turning up to *her* kid's football games? There's no more paper in there. Hang on."

"It's okay, I've got some tissues. Someone should really say something to Barbara."

I pulled Rupert's door open. The blue-eyed woman stood frozen with another. She dropped a packet of tissues to the floor.

"I think you just did. It's a shame we can't all be as charitable as Audrey, isn't it?" I snapped. My hands shook at my sides. I pushed the women aside and ran down the stairs. I threw open the front door and ran as fast as I could until I was out of breath. I crouched over for a minute before dragging my tired body the rest of the way home.

Dear Aiden,

The answering machine flashed at me as I went downstairs this morning. I pressed play.

"Hi Barbara, what happened to you yesterday? Cassandra said she saw you leave in a hurry. Is everything okay? Anyway, Oliver is a little miffed that you didn't show up to walk Saada with him this morning, so I just thought I'd check in on you. Give me a ring when you can."

She'd called me. She was worried about me. Someone was worried about me. I snatched up the phone and dialled her back. I took a seat on the stairs and began scratching at some flaking paint on the wall. The phone rang for what felt like an eternity before someone finally answered.

"Hello? I FOUND IT! IT WAS IN OLI'S ROOM! Hello?" I put the receiver back to my ear after the shout.

"Rupert?"

"Yes. Who's this?" Rupert responded, but then immediately turned his attention to his brother. "Mum's gonna be so mad at you, Oli. It's always in your room."

I heard Oliver's voice argue something in the background and a scuffling over the receiver.

Oliver had won the battle.

"Hello? Hello who's this?" Oliver asked.

"It's a girl! MUM! OLIVER'S ON THE PHONE WITH HIS GIRLFRIEND!" I heard Rupert scream in the background.

"Get lost, Rupert! Hello? Is anyone even there?"

There was a scuffling again and a door slamming shut, before peace.

"Oliver, it's Ms. Bridges."

"Oh hi, Ms. Bridges. Where were you this morning? I was waiting for you outside, forever."

"I know, your mum told me. I wanted to apologise, Saada was sick last night, so I don't think taking her across the forest would have been a good idea."

There was thumping on his bedroom door. I could hear Rupert crying out in the background.

"Oh no, is she okay? Are we going to take her to the vet?"

Are *we?* My heart jumped at the question. The thumping sounded again in the background, followed by a deeper voice than Oliver's little brother's. I heard Jeffrey in the background.

"It's Ms. Bridges, she called to talk to *me.*"

"No, she didn't, Oliver. Your mum called her earlier. Give me the phone."

Oliver whined.

"Hi, Barbara. How's tricks?" Jeffrey had finally won the battle. "I think Audrey is in the back garden. Give me a sec. You enjoy the barbecue yesterday? It got a little out-of-hand, didn't it?" A chuckle. "Wait, here she is. It's Barbara."

"Hello? Barb? No, it's fine, Dear. Could you just carry on with the barbecue? I'll do the rest later. Barbara? You there? Hang on; I'm going to go back inside. The signal isn't great out here. There, you should be able to hear me better now. Are you okay?"

"Hey, Audrey. Yes, yes, I'm fine. Sorry for just taking off like that yesterday. I wasn't feeling so good, and I didn't want to make a scene. Maybe a little too much whisky in the morning." I forced a laugh and picked off a piece of paint as big as my hand.

Whoops.

"No need to apologise, Barbara, I was just worried about you. Plus, I had a drunk Cassandra on my hands saying it was her fault because she'd knocked wine all over you. Your shirt is hanging up on the line by the way. Don't let me forget that."

"Thanks for that. Saada and I have both come down with something. Although, I doubt she's suffering from too much whisky for some reason. Anyway, I think we're going to take it easy today, would you mind..."

"Please, Dear. Look it's still covered in grease. It needs to be left to soak. Sorry, Barb, what were you saying? We're still cleaning up from yesterday."

"I just hoped you could tell Oliver I'm sorry about this morning?"

"Of course! Do you want to speak to him?"

"No. I mean, I do, but I'd rather just get back to bed. I can't handle my drink anywhere near as well as I could in my glory days." I picked another piece of paint off the wall.

"Okay, I'll tell him for you. Do you think you'll be able to come by tomorrow? Jeffrey and I were actually hoping to go and look at some new garden furniture. It'd be great if we could time it for when you're out with Oliver. Maybe Rupert could join, too?"

Was that them needing us, Aiden? Perhaps it had taken less time than I'd initially thought, but I'm pretty sure that tomorrow morning, when the two of them are out looking at garden furniture, we will be responsible for the boys. *Our boys.*

"Of course. I can stop by around nine?" I turned my back to the flaking paint. "Rupert knows he's always welcome with us and I'd be more than happy to help."

"MUM! HE'S DOING IT AGAIN!" One of the boys cried out in the background.

"Perfect. Thanks so much, Barbara, I owe you one. See you tomorrow."

"See you..." she'd already hung up. I brushed the paint off the bottom few stairs and kicked the larger chunks towards the shoe pile to deal with later. I went back upstairs and slept until early afternoon. I deserved it. We all did.

Dear Aiden,

I took the boys across the forest this morning. I was outside their place at 8:50, greeted by a flurry of thank yous from the entire family. The boys were dressed head to toe in what was clearly their outdoors wear. Nothing matched. Anything that was once white is now a faint yellow or brown and there are a few stains ingrained in their clothes that I imagine are now an accepted part of the outfit.

We headed to the forest all smiles and excitement. Saada led the way, pulling hard on her lead, much to a struggling Rupert's surprise. Rupert, bless him, had attached a multi-coloured string to his glasses so they would stay on his head. We paraded through the forest at such a great pace that I'm surprised I was able to keep up with the younger legs among me that splashed through all-year-round puddles and kicked up piles of leaves that the wind would never reach. We crossed paths with other families, other dog walkers, and other children. We waved our hellos and stopped to chat on occasion. I could tell people presumed we were a family and I let them. I wasn't going to complicate anything for them. I haven't done anything wrong. Let them think what they like. Let them think we are one big happy family. Today we are. Me and my boys.

I made them both packed lunches. We sat on top of the hill just outside the forest where the cars pottering along on the motorway looked no bigger than ants. We devoured peanut butter and jam sandwiches along with orange slices, jelly cubes and chocolate.

We talked about everything and nothing at the same time. It was idle chatter, but it was consistently speckled with laughter. I know the boys enjoyed themselves. After lunch, we threw a Frisbee to Saada across the rolling field and watched her dismal attempts to catch it. It was a scene fit for a film, if it weren't for Saada's shocking lack of coordination. Instead of cheering, we winced as the Frisbee hit her square in the head.

We were out for around four hours in total. I eventually brought the boys back, fresh-faced and caked in dried mud. Audrey opened the door and burst out laughing.

"Jeffrey! Come and look at this. I don't know who these children are on our doorstep, but they couldn't possibly be ours." She stood with that stance that Rupert had so casually adopted, her head tilted slightly to one side, one hand on her hip and the biggest grin on her face.

Jeffrey joined. "Woah! Who are you and what have you done with my boys?" he asked.

The boys both rolled their eyes.

"Are you going to let us in or what?" Rupert asked, a smile playing across his face.

"I'm not sure if I should. Our sons might not be happy if we rent their rooms to strangers."

"Dad! Come on, it's us and you know it!" Rupert squealed.

Audrey finally gave in. "Go 'round the back you two and kick off as much of the mud as you can on the way. No shoes past the patio doors, please." The boys began heading off.

She turned to me. "Thanks so much for taking them, Barbara. Umm, boys, are you forgetting something?"

They turned back, their eyes wide. They both ran to me and threw their arms around me. I put my arms in the air at first. I've never been shown this much affection. I didn't know what to do with it. After a brief pause, I relaxed a little and then laughed, peeling them off me. I didn't want to upset Audrey. I'd never seen her get a goodbye like this.

"Thanks for looking after us, Ms. Bridges," Rupert said.

"Yeah, and thanks for lunch, Ms. Bridges."

They ran off, and I looked up at Audrey who was raising an inquisitive eyebrow at me.

"Lunch?"

I blushed. "Hardly. We just had sandwiches and a few snacks each. I wasn't sure how long we'd be out, so I thought it best I come prepared."

"Barbara, you really didn't have to." She smiled at me and Jeffrey nodded his goodbye, heading back inside as we heard the boys bickering from the back of the house. "But, thank you all the same. That's really kind of you."

"You're welcome, I enjoy their company. They're great kids."

She nodded, and an awkward silence fell among us. "Well, thanks again, Barbara. See you tomorrow?"

"Sure."

She closed the door gently. I stood on the doorstep for a moment. Just like that, my blissful afternoon as a family member was over. I hadn't done anything out of term, had I? I don't think so. I replayed that scene in my head over and over on the walk home. Why had that awkward silence fallen between us? It reminded me of the end of a date from one of those old romantic comedies. The man walks the woman home and the woman stands fiddling with her keys on the doorstep before finally inviting the man in for a nightcap. Did Audrey think I was waiting to be invited in, that I wasn't quite done? I guess I'll find out tomorrow. But after those few seconds of awkward, I don't think I want to see Audrey tomorrow or maybe even the day after that.

Dear Aiden,

The boys hugged me through my dreams last night and I woke up feeling warm and full. It took me a while to realise why I'd woken up so early. I pulled at the threads of my dreams, unravelling more of what happened. I remembered looking up from the boys' heads. It came back to me. No matter what direction I turned I would see Audrey standing there. She had been in that famous Harper stance, one hand on hip, with fangs for teeth and eyes hot red.

Audrey didn't come to the door this morning as usual. Something has changed between us and I'm not entirely sure how I let that happen. Today it was just Oliver and me. I asked him if his mother was okay, but he said she was just really busy this morning. I wanted to know if that was Oliver's answer or if that's what his mother had told him to say. I didn't want to risk that question making it back to Audrey. So, I kept my mouth shut and let the first half of my dream repeat itself in my head.

Oliver peeled me away from my thoughts every now and again. It's his birthday next week and he couldn't be more excited about it. He's having a party in his back garden and asked if I'd be able to come. I told him I couldn't make it before he'd even told me the date. I knew exactly what would happen at the party.

I imagined the whispers on the wind as I walk by the pack of hyenas. I imagined the cackles at my back, their jaws snapping at my pride. I told Oliver that we'd celebrate with just me, him and Saada. It would be better that way. There's just one thing I need to do before his big day.

1ˢᵗ July

Dear Aiden,

It's your big brother's birthday today. His gift is wrapped and sitting on the kitchen table. When we were younger, your aunty Fi and I used to set up birthday mornings for your nana. We'd collect all of her presents and lay them neatly on a tray. We tried our best to cook her breakfast as well. We were too young to do much in the kitchen, but your Grandpa wasn't much better when it came to cooking. We always managed to put something edible and colourful together, though. Fi and I would head out down the road and pick flowers from our neighbours' front gardens to decorate our offerings. We'd knock gently on her bedroom door and slip in, singing *Happy Birthday* at the top of our lungs. Looking back on it now, your nana had probably been awake for hours. They were both early risers, but she'd hear us clattering about downstairs and would play along until we managed to get our things together. In her last few years with us, we started cooking her breakfast again, and we still adorned the tray with flowers. Yet, we wouldn't wake her with song; every day was her birthday in those years. Every day we were blessed to still have her, and we showered her with love and flowers.

Perhaps I've gone a little overboard, but it will be worth it to see the look on Oliver's face as he unwraps it. I just want everything to be perfect for him. I'm going to pick him up now and take him for a walk before his party. Jeffrey told me we'd actually be doing them a favour by getting him out of the way for a little while. Apparently, they have a few surprises to set up for him. That's fine by me, that's fine by us. I'll let you know how it goes. I love you. I love us.

Dear Aiden,

I took Oliver to the park. Not the main one on Manford Way, it's too busy there. We went to the smaller one at the end of Arrowsmith Road. No one ever goes there. The morning was hot, and the breeze was welcome. A perfect day for a party. Audrey was nowhere to be seen again this morning and, as I suspected, Oliver told me she was busy. I'll allow that today, though. She has a lot to prepare for our little boy.

I greeted Oliver at the door. "Shall we, Mr. Harp?"

"We shall," he replied. His eyes were already glued on the wrapped parcel poking out of my bag-for-life. He greeted Saada on his knees, and I saw his eyes flit from Saada to me.

"Let's head to the park today, Oliver, I have a surprise for you."

"Is it wrapped in blue paper and living in a shopping bag?"

"Correct." I smiled at him, and he beamed up at me. What I wouldn't give to see that smile every day for the rest of my life.

He walked with a spring in his step and whipped up Saada's lead like he was riding a horse and cart.

"Giddy-up Saada, we've got surprises to see."

The two trotted a little ahead of me while I struggled to keep up. Oliver turned left at the end of his street.

"Oli, not that one. Let's head to the little park at the end of Arrowsmith."

"There's a park there?"

Perfect.

"Yep."

"Sure." He spun on his heels and started heading up towards Arrowsmith with poor Saada being dragged behind him like a rag doll.

We eventually reached the park. It isn't much, really. There's a set of toddler swings in the corner, a roundabout that doesn't go around anymore, some sad looking monkey bars, and an elephant on a giant spring. I took a seat on the bench where I pictured we would sit and patted the space next to me. Oliver obliged and sat close to me, his face inches from mine, his smile blinding me and eclipsing my world.

Just as I hoped, we were alone. The park was on a small patch of green and overlooked by four and a half houses across the road. No one would be able to make out who we were, though, as we were hidden by the monkey bars and the arms of trees stretching free from the forest. It's a sanctuary. Our sanctuary. An image of me pushing you on the swings popped into my mind, and I quickly shook it out. I needed to stay present for this.

"So," I said, patting my hands on my lap, playing ignorant to the elephant in the room—or in the park for this matter.

"So," he repeated, squirming next to me, his fingers running rings around each other in his lap.

"So..." I could draw this out forever. "I heard it's someone's birthday today."

He nodded. "You heard correctly."

"I heard," I continued, as I brought the present out of the bag and onto my lap. "that someone is turning 13." His hands were rotating quicker in his lap, his eyes glued on the present. "You know, in my family, 13 is a big birthday to celebrate. You're officially a teenager."

"I am." He was desperately trying to focus on what I was saying but he could barely make out a reply.

"So, keeping to family traditions, I decided to get you a gift to match the occasion. I wanted to get it for you earlier, but it's *strictly* 13 and up." He kicked his legs up in joy and scrunched up his face before covering it with his hands. I moved the parcel onto his lap. He uncovered his face and held the parcel in his hands.

"Can I open it now?"

"Of course! It's yours."

He tore at the paper before I even managed to finish my sentence. The sheets were thrown to the ground as he forgot where we were. Rotating the parcel in his lap, he tore layer after layer away. I double-wrapped it so I could savour this moment as long as possible.

"No way!" He held the Lego firefighters' set at arm's length. "No. Fricking. Way."

"Oliver!" I scolded.

"Sorry." He threw his hand over his mouth. "I've wanted this *forever*. You remembered!" He bit down on his finger, turning it white.

"Of course, I remembered."

"But how did you even find it? It's super rare!"

"I have my ways." I tapped my nose. The truth is I'd been bidding online for it throughout the last week. I ended up paying far more than I should have for it just to outbid a collector, but it was worth it. It was all worth it now. He was still holding it in front of him and shaking his head in disbelief.

"I can't wait to get home and start on it. Ugh, I don't even want to have the party anymore! I just want to start with this!" He shook it in his hands.

"Don't be silly, Oliver. You'll still want your party as soon as you get home. This isn't going anywhere, don't worry."

"Thank you, thank you, THANK YOU!" He jumped off of the bench, put the Lego set down and threw his arms around me. I hugged him back immediately, and we stayed like that for a while. He kept on whispering his thanks into my ear. I felt incredible. My eyes began to tear up. I pulled him away from me and dabbed my eyes.

He looked at me, concerned. "Is everything okay?"

"Yes." I nodded. "I'm just happy you like it."

"I don't like it, I LOVE it!" He shouted again and hugged me once more. I could get used to this. I laughed into his curls; he smelt of mangoes. I let a few tears escape. They were happy tears though, Aiden. Tears I haven't seen or felt in a very long time.

"Gosh, what's the time? We better get you back. You, Sir, have a party to prepare for."

"I do, indeed." He said, his smile never faltering for a moment. He picked up his Lego firefighters' house once more and shook his head again. We headed back, his present cradled in front of him. He kept nuzzling his head into my arm and whispering how happy he was. He couldn't believe I'd found one.

We finally reached his front door and Oliver rang the doorbell. It opened almost immediately.

"Oh, I thought you were the clown." Audrey said, putting a hand on her hip and smiling down at her son.

"Mum! I said no clowns. I'm not four anymore." Audrey laughed, a hearty, full-bellied laugh. The gratification we get out of humiliating our kids is perhaps a little scary at times.

"Of course, I didn't get you a clown, silly. You're enough of a clown for me." She tussled Oliver's hair and to my surprise he let her. Clearly, he was in a good mood. She finally noticed the Lego set.

"Oliver! That isn't from Ms. Bridges, is it?" He nodded his head vigorously at her. Audrey's mouth opened and closed for a moment. "Head into the garden and see if your dad needs help with anything, will you?"

He saluted his mother and ran inside.

"Shoes!" she called over her shoulder. "And, don't even think about opening that today. I know you won't leave your room for weeks." Audrey folded her arms and turned towards me. Saada pulled at the lead, edging to get going.

"You really didn't need to get him that, Barbara. I looked into it once. It's incredibly expensive. You've probably spent more on him than Jeffrey and I. You're going to make me look like a bad mother."

I blushed. I hadn't intended to do that at all. *Had I?*

"Seriously, Barbara. I actually think it's too much. How much did you spend? Let me pay you back for some of it at least." I shook my head and held up my hand.

"Honestly, Audrey, it's fine. I have a friend that works in the toy store on Manford Way. Friends in high places." I winked at her.

"I actually tried to get him that for his last birthday. I looked for weeks but everywhere was sold out or had them way over my budget." She shook her head and looked down at her feet. "Barbara, I've been speaking to some of the girls. They've not been the most supportive of my idea to let you look after the boys. I've always brushed it aside, to be honest. They don't know you like I do, and they certainly don't know you as well as the boys do. But now this? I think the boys could start getting confused. I think it might be best if we cool things off for a while."

It sounded like a bad break up.

"Cool what off, Audrey?"

"Everything with the boys. Well, more so with Oliver. He asks about you a lot..."

I suppressed a smile and I felt my cheeks flushing as she finished "...and you're not even family. I just...I think we may be overstepping boundaries here."

"Oh..." I started to feel sick. I crossed one arm across my belly and put the other hand on my mouth. My brow furrowed like it does when I try to read something far away.

"This isn't easy for me either, Barbara, believe me. But seeing that in his hands. It's too much. It's all too much."

I nodded. I didn't trust myself to say anything more.

Shouldn't we be asking Oliver if he thinks it's too much?

"Look, I've got tonnes to do before the guests arrive. Please..." She took a few breaths and squinted down the street before eventually locking her eyes onto mine. "Don't come by again."

The wind had been knocked out of me. I'd just spent a small fortune on our little boy only to be told I'm not allowed to see him again. Saada whined at my heels and tugged on the lead once more. I let her take me. My eyes stayed on Audrey as I was pulled away. That was not how I expected my afternoon to turn out.

Saada walked me home. When I got inside, I kicked off my shoes and sulked into my bedroom. I grabbed the Lego wizard from my bedside cabinet and held it to my chest until I eventually fell asleep.

Dear Aiden,

I haven't seen Oliver for a month now. How can anyone go from seeing someone they love so dearly every day to not seeing them at all? I wonder if he thinks of me as much as I think of him. I wonder what his mother told him. Did she lie to him about me? The summer heat is making me sweat. I spend most of my days in my bedroom with the fan on full blast.

I need Oliver back in my life. I need a reason to wake up in the morning. Instead, I just lay in my bed and watch the fan spin overhead. I imagine what it would feel like if it fell from the ceiling...if the blades came spinning down onto me and sliced me to pieces. I wonder if I would scream. I wonder if anyone would care.

When I was about six months pregnant with you, I took a day trip to London with your aunty Fi. We were going to go baby clothes shopping, but we ended up shopping for your aunty instead. We were queuing at a checkout. The sun was as hot as it is today. People were huffing and puffing and fanning themselves with whatever they could. The line was long, and the staff were slow. The heat made me irritable. There was a father with a child and shopping baskets a few people back from us. The child couldn't have been older than 12 months old. The little thing was screaming. I mean, really going for it and throwing little fists of anguish into the air. The father didn't have a clue what to do. He was juggling a child in one arm and managing four baskets filled with clothes in the other. He kept cooing to the child, trying to soothe him. He tried blowing on its face to cool it down. My heart went out to him. Others were exchanging nasty looks and tutting in hope the child would take the hint and quit the noise. I had nothing but understanding for this family I didn't know.

A woman whom I presumed to be the child's mother came rushing up, edging her way past people in the queue, apologising profusely as she went with a three-pack of mustard yellow underwear in her hands. She dug a black set out of one of the bags her partner was carrying and threw it into the little tubs you see at the checkouts filled with impulse buys. She quickly took the child from the father's arms.

The father looked relieved. He flexed his arm, gave it a shake, and then split the shopping between them. The baby silenced instantly, wound like web in his mother's love. The attitude in the queue changed and people forgot the sweat running down their backs and cooed along with the family at the baby's adorable laugh. I hoped that you'd need me as much as that in the future. That you'd come into my arms and just like that, you would be at peace. Not just at peace, but happy.

"Next, please," the cashier called, and you kicked me into gear.
Happy Birthday, Love.

7th September

Dear Aiden,

It has been 37 days since I last saw Oliver. I have gone through various lows. I was about to write ups and downs, but there have been no ups. There have been days when the lows weren't quite as low, but I am always below surface level. I am always drowning. But, today there is hope. Today is the day the schools open their doors once more.

I woke up early. I decided a long time ago that this was my only hope of getting Oliver back. I prepared his packed lunch yesterday; I just needed to put his sandwich together. Since our mornings with Oliver, I haven't been walking Saada even half as much as I should have been, so Saada has got thicker around the edges. Her belly has plumped like a ripe fruit and her gait is slower. She started whizzing about the garden mid-August in what looked like a desperate attempt to stay in shape. The heat eventually got to her, too.

I grabbed Saada's lead from the coat hook, and suddenly she was full of energy, just like the old times. I say old times as if it were that long ago.

"Are you ready to go see Oliver?" She barked and sprinted into the kitchen and back. I'm not sure if she picked up Oliver's name or if she was just as desperate to get out of the house as I was.

We waited on the corner of Arweneck Avenue from 8:00. Every time someone walked past, I pretended to be fixing Saada's lead. Luckily no one walked past more than once, as I didn't have a Plan B.

I heard the boys before I saw them. They were laughing together as if nothing had happened in the past month to make them act otherwise. I felt such disappointment towards Oliver. I thought I meant more to him. I didn't realise he would just carry on with his life. I didn't realise he'd let his world keep on turning even if I'd forced mine to a stop.

I turned away from them as they passed on the other side of the road. I didn't want to look at him. Saada, on the other hand, had a very different idea. She caught wind of Oliver and yanked at her lead with a force I hadn't felt before. I let go and she sprinted across the road, barking. Oliver spun around. I couldn't work out the expression on his face or figure out what he was saying to Saada. I could hear that his voice was a little higher than usual as he knelt down to greet her. His friends stood by him, not kneeling—just waiting. He looked up, his hands wrapped around Saada's face, and his eyes locked onto mine. I saw his mouth move and his friends looked up to me before turning to leave. I thought he would get up and turn to leave with them. Instead, he picked up Saada's lead and crossed the road towards me. His eyes stayed on mine. I felt the back of my head grow hot and sweat began to run down the creases in my neck. I held the lunch box in front of me as my shield, my checkered hat.

"I finished it," he said. "It's incredible." His voice was deeper.

"I'm pleased. I, I made you lunch. If you want it."

"Mum told me it's best if we give you some space for a bit."

He'd shot up over summer.

"Take the lunch, Oliver, please."

He took it from me and quickly slipped it into his rucksack.

"Will you see me after school?"

"I've got practice." His blazer exposed the whites of his wrists.

"Please, Oliver?"

He sighed. "Fine, I'll meet you in our park."

Perhaps if I hadn't made him lunch that morning Oliver never would have met me in the park after school. Perhaps if I hadn't taken Saada with me, he never would have noticed me.

Oliver came to the park that afternoon and many afternoons after that. We spent about 30 minutes in the park each day. We couldn't spend too much longer or Audrey would get suspicious. I continued making his lunches and he continued eating them. Of course, we couldn't tell anyone about our meetings. I don't think people would understand our relationship. No one understands it apart from us. That's okay with me. We have no one to impress. I gave that up long ago.

Dear Aiden,

This morning Oliver and I were both wrapped up as tight as Christmas presents. I was wearing my black knee length coat with its deep pockets that once housed Oliver's hat. I pulled the silk sash tight around my waist. Audrey has finally updated Oliver's wardrobe. She's gone from one extreme to the other. Whereas after summer Oliver was all wrists and ankles, he's now drowning in a duffel coat two sizes too big for him. His gloved fingertips barely poke out of the end of his sleeves. He was wearing the hat that brought the two of us together, his curls spilling out around his face. I smile every time I see it. I think Oliver knows I like him wearing it.

We'd been playing "And Then..." and had got so carried away with the idea of Jeffrey dressed up as an elf for Christmas that I only realised how far we walked by the time it was too late. The weather has grown cold too quickly this year, and the air snaps at your cheeks like piranhas in a river. The rooftops are already dusted with snow. We breathed ice smoke in front of our faces, which briefly hazed our rosy red cheeks. We were laughing so hard.

Everything happened at once. My foot lost its grip on the ice. I hit the ground. I must have looked such a picture, still laughing and smiling as I fell, my face rushing to greet the gravel. There was a deafening crack. My skull shook. I saw black. My hands were still in my pockets. I squirmed like a fish on land, pulling my face away from the pavement, looking through patches of black. I saw a thick red river cutting its way through the ice like strawberry sauce on lemon sorbet. My head throbbed and my stomach rumbled. *My stomach.* I pulled my hands out of my pockets, and instead of assessing the damage done to my face, they rushed to my stomach. I heard someone calling my name but something else was louder.

All I could hear, and wanted to hear, was your rattle—your music that never was. I landed face first, but my belly hit the ground next and I was winded. All I could think about was you, Aiden. A voice calling my name broke through our music.

"Barbara? Barbara, Are you okay?" A pair of hands reached under my arms. Little hands lifting and turning me so that I sat on my backside. I blinked through the darkness and Oliver came back into view. Parts of his face were blotted out. My brain filled the dark parts with images of you.

"Barbara? Oh crap, you're bleeding."

"Aiden?" The boy looked confused.

"No, Barbara. I'm *Oliver.*"

"Aiden." I pulled off a glove and put a pale hand to his face, your face. I didn't know how much of what was whose. I blinked a few more times and Oliver's face bloomed through images of you. The morning was hushed, more so than any blanket of ice and snow could achieve. I looked around. We'd reached the school gates. Parents were staring at us. Whispers began to mist the air. None of them made a move to help. I looked back to Oliver. He was scanning my face, and his eyes were dancing from each of my features. I shook my head again. My hand was still on his cheek, your cheek.

"You called me, Barbara?" I put my hand to my mouth and coughed. I spat blood. My tongue traced the inside of my mouth. Something wasn't right. The metallic taste of blood overwhelmed my senses. My tongue ran along my top row of teeth and there, at the front, it caught. It played in a crevice where part of my tooth used to be. I spat again into my hand, swimming around was part of my front tooth, white as a snowdrop in a sea of red.

"You called me Barbara?" I looked back to Oliver.

"Sorry, Ms. Bridges, but your tooth. We should take you..."

"Please," I offered my hand up to him as he helped me to my feet. I must have looked like a chunkier version of *Bambi* on ice.

"Please," I repeated. "Call me Barbara." I tried to smile, but my gum caught on the jagged edge that had become my front tooth.

The parents around us were not even attempting to be discreet. You could practically see our names flitting from mouth to ear. I tried to compose myself.

"Get yourself into school, Oliver, before the second bell goes." Each word sounded fuzzy, and my head was pounding.

"But, Ms. Bridges?" He looked as though he were chewing something foul as he tried to say my name, despite it coming so naturally to him earlier. "But Barbara, I want to make sure you're alright."

Parents started edging closer to us now, like hyenas moving in on the weak. I gave him a reassuring pat on the shoulder.

"I'll see you tomorrow, Oliver. Come on now, Saada, let's go home." My words came out as if I had a lisp. I didn't want to spit blood for fear of looking anti-social. I took a few gulps of metal and gagged at its taste on the back of my throat. I turned away from Oliver, making an overly exaggerated effort to get Saada to come with me. I just needed something to do. Something to make me seem more human.

We started walking away, and my ears were burning. I swayed a little; scared I was going to go down once again. I risked a quick look over my shoulder as I walked away from the school. Just as I feared, Oliver was standing there staring at me. He hadn't left the spot where I'd fallen, and little specks of blood lay at his feet like blooming poppies.

Surrounding parents looked on with their mouths open wide enough to catch flies if any have survived this late in the year. I turned away. Images of Oliver's face and yours blurred my vision. I haven't heard from you in so long, Aiden, and yet there you were.

You always will be.

The walk home was hazy. I received some concerned looks from pedestrians, but either out of fear or courtesy no one approached me. Saada whined at my heels; I think she knew something wasn't right with me. She kept licking the hand that I hadn't bothered to re-glove. I skidded a few more times on the ice, not one 100 percent confident with my body's ability to manoeuvre. I didn't dare return my hands back to my coat pockets. I kept them out at my sides, just a fraction, as if tightrope walking.

I spat blood into bushes when I knew no one was looking. But I felt so disgusting doing it that, more often than not, I swallowed the blood instead. It tasted foul, but I didn't want to ruin this white blanket that coated our streets. Upon reaching home, my body relaxed a little. The ice was thinner here and the faint late morning sun had melted the worst of it away. Little rainbow pools of oil and old ice swelled in the pavement's dimples.

The answer machine flashed at me as I closed the front door. I ignored it and rushed upstairs to the bathroom mirror. My tongue traced the new contours of my mouth over and over again. I had this horrible vision of looking like a pirate with an entire tooth missing. I laughed a little as the vision evolved into me with my missing tooth, along with an eye patch and a hook for a hand at your second birthday party.

Yes, that will be the theme for it—it will be a pirate-themed party. We'll have an alligator as a piñata, a special pirate rum punch for the adults, and hundreds of golden coins hidden around the garden for you and your friends to find. Perhaps you will be a bit too young to care about finding treasure. Perhaps you won't quite grasp the concept, but the parents will and that's important.

The natural light in the bathroom didn't quite filter through the frosted window, so I turned the bulb on. I gripped the sink and spat the last mouthful of blood into the bowl. I cleared my mouth and looked up, grimacing in the mirror so I could see the full effect of my fall. Two dried streams of blood fell from each nostril and encased my lips. A small graze had hatched across my forehead, nose, and chin. Tiny little bits of gravel were caught in drying rivers of blood that ran down my face. I smiled into the mirror, wishing my lips were fuller and covered more. The inside of my top lip briefly caught my chipped tooth and tore open a little. My front right tooth was half the size it once was. It had two jagged edges on either side, like fangs.

I took my coat off, threw it in the tub and tied my hair back as if that would help the situation. Mummy looked awful. My gums ached, my cuts stung, and I wanted nothing more than to sleep for the rest of the day. Instead, I popped a couple of painkillers and sucked on a jelly cube before confronting the mirror once more. I practised smiling with my mouth shut. I tried to smile using only my lips. I constantly looked like I was being patronising or sarcastic. I practised my greetings in the mirror, my language. I practised how I would start presenting myself to people until I could see our dentist and get a crown fitted. I practised saying your name. Maybe we'll get a lollipop later if we're on our best behaviour. There's someone at the door. I'll write to you later, Aiden.

Dear Aiden,

Oh God, what have I done? It was Oliver at the door. How did everything go wrong so quickly? I tiptoed downstairs and the knock resounded in the hallway. The flashing red of the answering machine cast a glow onto the walls that made it look as though I had walked into a crime scene. If the knock hadn't been so persistent, I would have guessed it was Aunty Fi at the door. I'd have guessed that she came crawling back, filled with apologies and jelly cubes. The knock sounded again. I pulled the lock back and slid the door open an inch or two, trying to cover as much of my mouth as possible, which is difficult to do behind a door.

"Oliver?"

He looked up at me, shyly, and then looked down the street. I pulled the door open and craned my neck outside, scanning the street with him.

"What is it? What's wrong?"

"I'm supposed to be in school, Barbara." He'd practised saying my name, I could tell, he said it like he was reciting a line for a school play.

"I was just..." He hesitated for a moment, suddenly obsessed with my faded welcome mat. "I left school after lunch. I was just worried about your face."

Pride bubbled up inside me, and it took all my strength to bite back a gappy smile. Finally, someone was looking out for me. Finally, I meant something to someone. But this was not right. I couldn't be responsible for him skipping school to come see me. I thought of the best way to convince him to go back. Maybe the head teacher wouldn't punish him too badly if he returned before the end of the school day.

"Oliver, do you want to come in?" Okay, so it didn't quite come out how I wanted it to. I had hoped to sound more authoritative, to put up a better argument that would send him running back to school with his tail between his legs. No such luck. I took another step back and opened the door. Oliver kept his eyes down. I could tell he hadn't thought this far ahead. His great escape from school had been an impulsive act. I couldn't help but remember our game.

Barbara Bridges opened her front door and gestured for Oliver Harp to come inside, and then...

I smiled a little at the ridiculous events that had just played out on my front doorstep. My thought trail began steaming away from reality. Images of Oliver in this house cascaded upon me.

Oliver's coat hanging up in the hallway, pairing up his socks from the wash load, his smell seeping into my sofa...

He shuffled in with his hands in his pockets and knocked clumps of fresh snow from his boots. He stood on the mat in the hall for a moment, shifting his weight from left to right.

Kissing his head as he leaves for school in the morning.

"Would you like a drink?"

Signing his name next to mine on Christmas cards.

He nodded, and I left him to his own devices in the hall as I scuttled off to the kitchen. My hands were shaking. I hadn't had anyone in my house since Aunty Fi left. Who knew all those months ago that picking up a stranger's hat would lead to this? I giggled a little at the almost hysterical situation.

Scrambling his eggs.

"Oliver? Do you drink tea?" I called.

Running his bath after dinner.

"One sugar, please."

I heard the creak of the stairs and I imagined him sitting down and sliding his boots off. I shook my head as I watched the kettle boil. One thud, then a second. I imagined his boots joining my cluster of shoes by the wall, a welcome addition to my collection. The kettle boiled as I heard the creak of the stairs once more. I pictured Oliver cautiously getting to his feet and sliding along my laminate floor towards the kitchen. I reached for the teacups. My hands wouldn't stop shaking. I reminded myself to breathe slowly. I poured sugar into the empty mugs. From the corner of my eye, I saw him slide in, and I moved away towards the fridge. I wasn't ready to see him in my house yet. I buried my head in the fridge because apparently my milk was that hard to find.

"Do you want a snack or anything? I've got Maltesers?"

"Just tea is good. Thanks, though."

At long last, I found the milk in the fridge door, just where I'd left it. I turned back to the tea, milk in hand, eyes transfixed on the mugs. I could see Oliver shifting by the door, the new boy in the playground. I placed the teacups onto saucers. I'd never done this before, but I felt it was an appropriate occasion to have teacups and saucers.

"Where's Saada?" Oliver shattered the silence with common ground on foreign turf.

"She's out in the garden digging up God knows what."

I looked at him. There he was, just as he looked that morning. Perhaps a little more dishevelled, but he was here, in our home. I kept feeling pride, Aiden. Of all the things I expected to feel, pride was not one of them. I felt proud that he was in our house, and prouder that he'd chosen to come here of his own accord. I felt proud that I managed to keep Barbara Bridges and Oliver Harp a secret from the big, bad world. I felt proud of myself, proud for being able to retain someone in my life for so long.

That was always the make or break with friends when I was young. Inviting friends home was always a deal breaker. You were inviting them into your most intimate space, laying your heart on the table and saying, "This is me, take it or leave it." Most of my friends never came back.

There I was, Aiden, in all my intimacy and at my most vulnerable. I was laying my heart, with one sugar, on the table. *Take it or leave it, Oliver.* He walked over to the kitchen table and sat down, not quite at ease but trying to be so. I was happy enough with that. I pulled a packet of biscuits out from the cupboard. I sat down opposite him, our knees faintly brushing against each other's.

"How did you know where I live?" I asked.

"I didn't, I remember you said the name of your road during one of our And Then games, so I just tried every house until I got yours."

"Oh, Oliver! How many houses did you try? Who answered their doors?"

"A couple of people answered. The ancient lady on the corner of your road really isn't very nice, is she?" I smiled, knowing exactly who he was talking about—Mrs. Dewley, renowned for her prying eyes. Oliver's face dropped as I saw his eyes notice my tooth, or lack of it.

"Barbara, I'm so sorry about what happened this morning."

I corrected my smile to a lip smile and shook my head.

"Don't worry, Oliver. It wasn't your fault." I took a sip of my tea. It felt like hot coals on my tooth and my head pounded. Oliver followed suit. He grimaced. I laughed. He smiled at me.

"What?" he giggled.

"You don't really like tea do you, Oliver?" I raised a questioning eyebrow at him over my steaming mug. He flushed red and looked down at his hands.

"I do! You just have different tea to mum's. It takes a bit of getting used to." As if to reassure me, he took another sip from his mug and looked up at me and smiled. "See? I'm used to it already."

I nodded and looked away. Out of the corner of my eye, I saw him grimace once again, unable to keep a neutral expression.

"Oliver, I've got juice if you'd like some instead? I won't be offended."

"Have you got orange?" he mumbled.

I couldn't hold back the laughter. Oliver looked at me, his face a Merlot red, which just made me laugh even more. He started to laugh, and before I knew it, we were in hysterics.

"I just copied what my dad always says whenever my mum offers him tea."

"I thought as much."

"Honestly, I don't think I'll ever like it. It's horrible. I don't understand why so many people drink it."

"You'll come 'round, My Love, everyone does." Oliver didn't look convinced. He pushed his teacup and saucer into the centre of the table.

"I'll get you that juice." The tension eased between us as Oliver came out of his shell and stopped pretending to be older than he was. I drank my tea and Oliver drank his juice. We chatted over biscuit crumbs and neglected china saucers. It was beautiful.

"Shall we bring Saada in? I'm sure she'll be more than happy to see you've come to visit."

"Sure," he said. I scooted over to the patio doors and slid them open. Saada's ears pricked up and she sprinted into the house, ran right past Oliver and into the hallway. A couple of seconds later, she returned with one of his boots and nuzzled it into his crotch.

"I think that's a sign if I ever saw one, Oliver. Come on, Saada, let's get you out of here. And you, Mr. Harp, should be heading home. Your mother will be wondering where you are. I appreciate you coming to check up on me, but this afternoon was a one off. Okay?"

"Yes, Ms. Bridges."

"What did I say?" I caught Oliver's smile and just laughed again, realising how much of a parent I sounded.

Oh, Aiden. Come back to me.

"I just need to grab my coat from the bath. Wait for me in the hall, okay?" He gave me that endearing puzzled look. I just shook my head and smiled. "Don't ask."

He grinned back as I ran upstairs. My stomach somersaulted on a bed of excitement. The afternoon could not have turned out more perfectly. I felt closer to Oliver than I ever had before. We had another little secret to add to our world. It strengthened us and severed ties to everyone else. It was perfect, Aiden.

I went to the bathroom and grabbed my blood-stained coat from the bath. I made a mental note to get it dry-cleaned as soon as possible. I caught my reflection in the mirror as I was leaving the bathroom. I swept my hair back in a fresh ponytail and pinched my cheeks a couple of times to give them a blush. I smiled, remembered my cracked tooth and changed to a lip smile; it was starting to feel a little more natural. Heading down the stairs, swinging my coat on, I heard Oliver mumbling something to Saada.

"Come on, Oliver, let's get you home," I said.

"I'd love to, but someone isn't too keen on the idea," he replied.

I looked at Saada. Her head bowed to the ground. Oliver stood with one boot in his hand.

"What have you done with my other boot, Saada? Come on, I need to get home." Oliver helplessly waved his boot in Saada's face. She took a sniff before walking to the living room door. She began whining and scratching at the floor.

"Saada, you know you're not allowed in there." She jumped up on her hind legs, placed her front paws on the handle, and used her weight to pull the handle down. The door swung open a little and she nuzzled her way into the living room. Oliver was quick to follow, intrigued.

"Oliver, wait." But it was too late. He was already in the living room.

"Woah...who are all the presents for?"

"Saada get out of there. Saada! Out!" I pushed past Oliver and headed towards Saada, whose head was buried among your baby shower gifts.

"Saada!" I screamed. I couldn't stop screaming.

"Those are Aiden's. Saada, out!" She kept rummaging, knocking over your gifts. I started crying. Her tail was wagging.

Oliver looked from me to Saada. I could see his mind whirring behind his eyes. He looked to Saada as her head emerged from behind your gifts. I was shaking uncontrollably. My fists clenched so tight that my nails began to pierce my palms. Saada came out with a football boot in her mouth.

"Hey, I used to have football boots just like that one. So did my brother." Oliver made his way towards Saada. "We used to love our boots. Grandpops bought them for us two Easters ago." He pulled the boot free of Saada's grip. "Grandpops said they were better than any chocolate egg. Except one day one of Rupert's boots went missing, Mum hit the roof, said that he'd been careless."

My heart was in my throat.

"Mum started having a go at Dad for letting us leave them out in the front." He idly pulled the tongue of the boot out. "We never understood why just one..." His eyes registered the handwriting and his brother's name.

I saw him catch his breath and swallow hard. The room was thick with silence. He looked up at me with that same confused look on his face that he gave me that day he was playing football on the green. But his eyes were sterner now. My mouth opened. Something needed to fill this silence, this vacuum. My heart seemed to have crushed my vocal chords.

"I'd better get going, Ms. Bridges." He dropped the boot and headed towards the door. I stood to the side to let him pass. I was rooted to the spot.

The front door slammed and broke my trance, and I ran to the window. I saw Oliver running down my driveway with only one of his boots in his hands. I went into the hall. His coat still hung from the hook. The red flashing light on the answering machine panicked me. I spun, not knowing where to go or what to do. I ran for the toilet, tearing my coat off as I moved up the stairs. I made the toilet just in time and threw up everything I'd consumed in the last couple of days. I heard Saada run up the stairs, then felt her nuzzle at my side. I looked across the toilet bowl; she had Oliver's other boot in her mouth.

"You ruined everything, you stupid bitch!" I hit her. Saada stood there, confused for a second. She dropped the boot and then headed back downstairs. I spent the rest of the evening over the toilet bowl, running my fingers along the lining of Oliver's boot.

I woke up in the early hours of the morning. Saada was nuzzling my side again, whining. My head pounded, and my mouth was dry. I must have been dehydrated from throwing everything up. I peeled my face off the toilet bowl and dragged my frame to the sink. The water ran cold and soothed my raw throat. My mind registered the total darkness that engulfed me.

We had been snowed in. I'd been in a coma-like state for weeks and with no one to adjust the heating, I feared we would be lost and forgotten in a snowy grave. After all who would notice if we went missing? I shook the thoughts from my head and tried to bring myself back to a logical way of thinking. I stumbled into the hall. The red light of the answer machine still bounced off the walls. I threw the light on and looked at the wall clock. It was 3:47 in the morning. I must have slept for about eight hours. My left leg was still numb from the way I'd pinned it between the rest of my body and the bathroom tiles.

My neck ached from the awkward angle at which I'd slept. My throat was beginning to dry up again and my head was in absolute agony. I couldn't get away from the stench of vomit. I groaned and stumbled back into the bathroom. Saada seemed to have lost all hope and was curled up under the sink, sleeping off her hunger. I turned on the shower and peeled off my winter layers. I stood, shivering, with one hand under the shower, waiting for the water to warm up and for me to feel something other than nothing. The water didn't seem to be getting any hotter, so

I climbed into the shower anyway. Finally, with the cold water piercing through the hairs on my head, I began to wake up. I looked up at the showerhead and let my mouth fall open, let the water fill my mouth. I could have stayed like that for hours. I opened my gullet and let the water soothe my throat. The water eventually heated up before running ice cold. My hands began to prune. Light was just beginning to sneak through the bathroom window. I got out of the shower and failed to find a towel. I didn't put any effort into looking for one, anyway.

I headed downstairs, nude. Little drops of ice water trailed off the contours of my body and hit the floor. I was raining. The creak of the third to last stair sent a shiver up my spine as memories of yesterday hit the front of my mind. I fell back onto the stairs, and they creaked just as they had for Oliver when he sat to take off his school boots.

"Oh, Oliver."

Images of him at the front door, glancing hesitantly back down the street. Images of him at the kitchen table laughing over a glass of orange juice and cold tea. Images of Saada and Oliver at the living room door.

Yesterday's events came rushing back to me. I moved into the living room, thick with disturbed dust motes. Shafts of fractured light filtered through the shutters. Your presents sat askew against the far wall and Rupert's football boot lay, lonely, yet centre stage. I tore away from the memories of Oliver that now clouded the living room's dreams of you. I went to the kitchen, to the drawer with the scissors. I walked into the hallway and sat on the creaky step. I lifted my top and began to cut in every day without you. My blood ran thick and bold, like stage makeup in a grand finale. Droplets of red chased their way down the stretch marks on my belly and dripped onto the hallway floor. The blood shimmered in the light of the answering machine. I went to press play.

"You have one new message." *No shit, Sherlock.*

"Message one." A long beep sounded in the hall followed by:

"Barbara? It's Fi. Honey? Are you home? Look, I'm sorry for walking out on you. I really am. I just...I'm not doing this over an answer machine. Call me, okay? Just, just call me."

Well, would you look at that, Love? You win some, you lose some. It looks like Aunty Fi has come crawling back, and for what she is lacking in jelly cubes she makes up for in apologies. I hit speed dial one and let the dial tone fill the silence in my head. I let the ringing push images of Oliver from my mind.

"Hello? Barbara? Love? Are you there? Can you hear me okay?" Your tiny hands wrapped around my heart, caressed it. It had been so long since I'd heard Aunty Fi's voice and I'd forgotten how much of you lay in it.

"Barbara? Speak to me, Love. Please?"

I heard the creak of springs from her mattress. I sat back on the stairs and allowed memories of Fi's voice fill my mind. I looked around the hallway. I pictured Fi pruning herself in the mirror by the door as I decided whether to leave my coat open or try and pull it over my seven-month bump and tie the sash on top. I wanted to wrap you up like the gift from above that you were. My hands flitted up to my stomach, half expecting Bump to still be there. They just found my open wounds, my reminder of days without you.

"I'm here, Fi."

"Oh, thank God. Are you okay? Can I come over?"

"Bring a bottle," I replied, more out of habit to the question rather than actual need.

"I'll bring two." Guilt riddled her voice and thickened her forced, lighthearted tone.

"Come over tonight around seven."

"Yes. Yes okay, I'll see you at seven. Oh, and Barbara?"

"Yes?"

"Barbara, I love you. You know that right?"

"I know." I should have said it back. I should have echoed her without hesitation. But right now, Aiden, Mummy seems to be struggling with comprehending exactly what love is.

I walked into the kitchen to tidy away the dishes that Oliver and I left behind the day before. With Fi's voice resounding in my head, memories of my pregnancy came rushing back as I began to wash up the cutlery in the kitchen sink. I grabbed a T-shirt and threw it over my head, letting it soak up the small amount of blood I drew with the scissors.

Four weeks: Me not quite making it to the toilet after a salmon and poached egg breakfast with Fi. Laughing with happiness as I threw it all up into the kitchen sink.

Sixteen weeks: Fi walking in and finding me with a stick of celery dipped into peanut butter. That same day, me sitting at the kitchen table rolling a cluster of pennies around in my hands before smelling my fingers. You gave me the oddest cravings.

Thirty-four weeks: Me trying to rest my dinner plate on your bump, just like they do in the movies. But the plate was too hot and your bump was too round. A river of hot beans quickly made their way down my side and I didn't try it again.

Saada's barks drew me from my daydreams as the doorbell chimed. I'd managed to clean the house a little, put on some fresh clothes and run a brush through my hair a couple of times. I'd practised a welcoming smile in the mirror but cringed every time I saw the gap in my teeth. I'd applied some heavy, clumpy mascara to try to draw the attention away from my gap tooth smile. I brushed my sweater down a few times and cringed as my hands brushed against my wounds.

Deep breaths.

Dear Aiden,

"Hi." Fi stood awkwardly on the welcome mat, clearly not convinced by its encouragement.

"Come in." I think this may have been the first time I've ever had to invite Fi in. Usually she bustles her way past me, kissing me on the cheek as she passes and pours a glass of wine before I even make it to the kitchen.

She reached into the black polythene bag that swung at her side and pulled out a bottle of our favourite rosé. I smiled a well-practised lip smile, but it felt strained. I was uncomfortable standing in her way despite having invited her in. My mind felt like it should be trying to cling to some kind of etiquette, yet my body clearly had other ideas. I brushed a stray hair behind my ear and reluctantly stepped to one side, swinging the door open as I went.

Fi looked around, cautiously, as if at a house viewing. She took in everything with virgin eyes. I looked around too. The hallway was dark. Fi loosened the heel of her boot with the other foot before bringing her leg up to pull it off. It's a habit our father had hated; the heel of Fi's boots always wore down twice as quickly as mine because she couldn't be bothered to undo her laces.

Her fingers lightly rested against the wall. Her eyes darted from the floor to the walls, eventually resting on the closed living room door. She knew your presents still slept beyond that door. She knew they were still unopened, just waiting for the day when you'd be back to collect them.

"Fi?" I waved a hand in front of her face and brought her down from your cloud. She made a grand effort at taking her coat off. An equally strained smile played across her face as she hung it on a peg above the shoe pile.

I glanced down. I'd thrown Oliver's boot into the shoe pile whilst I was cleaning up this afternoon. Memories of you were so strong I hadn't even noticed I'd done it. Now it was nestled between last summer's flip-flops and my "out, out" wedges that hadn't made it "out, out" since before you. I thought Fi may have noticed, but when I looked up her eyes were on Oliver's coat. Her brow knotted in confusion.

"Head into the kitchen. I'll be there in a sec." Fi nodded, and with her eyes down, she stiffly headed into the kitchen. Her knees clicked at this new, unnatural rhythm she tried to pass off as walking.

I grabbed Oliver's boot and the coat and took the stairs two at a time. I pushed my door open and threw everything onto my bed. I turned to go but had second thoughts. Saada had a knack for opening doors recently and I couldn't handle explaining myself again, especially to Fi. I ran back into my room, opened my bed-side cabinet and tucked Oliver's boot at the back, behind a pack of vanilla tea lights. I hung Oliver's coat in my wardrobe in between suits I can't remember wearing. Closing the door, I left my hand on the wood for a moment and took a breath, preparing myself for a reunion in my kitchen with a stranger that I must call my sister.

Fi had tucked her feet up on the kitchen chair and was sitting cross-legged. Her arms were loosely crossed in her lap and everything about her screamed uncomfortable. The bottle of rosé sat unopened and lonely in the middle of the kitchen table, it looked vulnerable with no half-filled wine glasses at its side. I walked over to the cupboard and pulled out two wine glasses. I could feel Fi's eyes on my back and my face began to blush. I felt clumsy, oaf-like, in my own home. I set the two glasses on the kitchen table with an awkward clatter. Fi reached forward a tentative hand and the click, click, click of the wine bottle opening rang through the kitchen. The glug, glug, glug that followed, as she poured each glass, echoed even louder. I sat down opposite and Fi slid a wine glass over to me.

"I don't know where to start." She shook her head at me as if disagreeing with her own statement. I think we both knew where she needed to start, but neither one of us was going to admit it first. We are each as stubborn as the other. We inherited that from our mother's side.

I raised the glass to my mouth, let the wine touch my tongue and lowered it back to the table. She bit her lip, went to speak, then bit her lip once more. I could see her chewing over her own thoughts. I imagined them tumbling around inside her head like the contents of a washing machine as she tried to pluck out the right thing to say, the right garment for the occasion.

"I'm sorry, Barbara. I am." That alone took a lot. I don't think she's ever apologised to me in her life. Even when we were younger and our mother used to make her apologise for something she was clearly in the wrong for, I'd get a barely audible grumble rather than a full-on apology. Our mother was always happy enough with that. The very fact that she had chosen now, at this point in our lives, to apologise to me was the very thing that pushed us further apart. We were strangers sitting across my kitchen table. The only thing we had in common was our choice in wine.

"I didn't plan on running off. I didn't even realise I'd packed until I zipped up my case. I never intended to leave you, Barbara, and certainly not for that long. I took the kids to Joey's summerhouse in Brighton. I just didn't realise how much of a strain it all was. I love you, of course." She paused and took a breath. "It was so painful watching you go through it all that I chose not to. I'm sorry, I know it was stupid, stupidly selfish, but I just couldn't watch you waste away. I think you relied on me too much."

I nodded the whole way through until she delivered that last sentence. I held the glass in two hands and raised it to my lips. I put the glass back down and began to twirl it by its stem on the table.

"I don't think I relied on you that much, Fi."

"Barbara, please."

"You picked me up a few times. That's hardly being totally dependent on you, considering."

She glanced down at my stomach. I crossed my arms over it. She sighed. We drank.

"It wasn't just picking you up, Barbara, it was constantly having to make sure you took your medication, attended doctor's appointments, paid your bills. I can't remember when I stopped being your sister and started being your caregiver." Her eyes went wide for a moment and she pursed her lips. "Sorry that came out a bit strong."

"And here I am thinking you came here to apologise. You seem to be going about it in the oddest of ways." My grip tightened on the stem of the glass.

She sighed. "What happened to us, Barb?" She picked up the bottle of wine and marched over to the sink. She poured the rest of the bottle down the drain. Fi turned to me with her hands on the rim of the sink and her back slouched.

You happened, Aiden. We both knew that.

"I don't know, Fi." I stood up and walked over to her at the sink. I hugged her, and we stood like that for a long time. We stayed like that until each time our bodies swayed a little, our spines clicked, or our knees cracked. I think I may have even fallen asleep on her shoulder for a while, if that's possible.

The last person who held me like that was the midwife at the hospital. I had just got back from emptying our locker. Our bag was packed, ready to head home, and your baby carrier was at my side. I sat on the bed that I'd dreamt of breastfeeding you on. The same bed that apparently couldn't house me a day more because there were patients that "needed it more." The nurse who took my hand the day I came in, expecting you, sat next to me on the bed and held my hand once more. I refused to let go of your bag of gifts. She squeezed my hand and brought me close to her. I remember she smelt of hand steriliser and apricots. She told me she was sorry, and she told me that she had lost her little brother before there was time to meet him. She told me that you were up there with him now. Have you met him yet, Aiden? His name was Samuel. His name *is* Samuel. I remember the doctor swooped into our ward and the nurse jumped off the bed, making a scene of helping me get my things together. I felt betrayed that she could change so quickly but I understood why she did. She squeezed my shoulder and sent us on our way.

"Barb? Honey?" Fi's gentle voice lured me out of the awkward shoulder slumber I'd fallen into.

"Mmm?"

"My legs have gone numb." I peeled myself off her shoulder and tried to wipe a bit of drool from her top before she noticed the dark stain. I tried to make it look like I was giving her an affectionate pat.

"You've drooled on my shoulder, haven't you?"

My eyes were watery, and I nodded—guilty as charged. I tried to hold back a smile but couldn't. My lips broke open and I saw bits of spittle fly across the space between our faces and seek sanctuary on Fi's skin. This just made me laugh even more. Fi noticed my gap tooth, her face horrified, and I couldn't help but laugh even harder. It felt so good to let it all out.

"Barbara. I'm sorry, but what the fuck happened to your tooth? Actually, what the fuck happened to your face, Barb?"

At that, I just laughed harder. I know it wasn't really a laughing situation but if I didn't laugh, I'd cry, and Mummy's wasted enough water recently. Fi looked at me, not quite knowing if I'd entirely lost the plot or whether she ought to be happy that I'm happy. Ignorance is bliss, right?

"I wish you hadn't poured that wine away now. I've got a lot to tell you."

I retreated back to the kitchen table and slipped into my seat. Smiling, I looked up at Fi and patted the table opposite me. She relaxed and took the invite. I put four fingers to my lips, curled my tongue and blew hard. A loud high-pitched whistle erupted, and I laughed again, cutting it short. It was enough, though. Saada came crashing down the stairs, skidding into the kitchen. She didn't change her pace as she sped into the kitchen, so she slid into the cupboards. There was a loud thud that should have shocked her a little, but Saada being Saada, she didn't feel a thing. She kept running on the spot for a moment before her paws eventually found grip and she charged in Fi's direction. Fi's face lit up as Saada jumped up onto her hind legs and put her front paws on Fi's lap while she leant forward trying to lick the perfume from Fi's neck.

"Saada. Saada down. It's alright. She's friendly. She's okay. Saada get down." I hustled Saada off and squatted over her, rubbing her stomach.

"Fi, this is Saada, my partner in crime, and the reason I am now a gap tooth."

"Nice to meet you, Saada." Fi put her hand out, Saada leant to one side and raised a heavy paw onto her palm. I went over to the cupboard to get her some food.

"Saada likes long walks in the park and is a recovering addict."

Fi played along. "Really? What was it? Alcohol? Drugs?" I shook my head.

"No, no, it's a lot worse than that. She was addicted to C-H-O-R-I-Z-O. It's been three weeks since her last relapse and we're really proud aren't we, Saada?"

"Chorizo!" I put my hand up to stop Fi from finishing the word, but Saada had already heard it.

26th November

Dear Aiden,

This morning was bright. I woke with the sun, naturally, and felt like I could conquer whatever the day threw at me. It always took me a while to orientate myself in the morning. My mind still flashed back to Oliver. Normally, I can't remember my dreams, but I can only guess that Oliver is still pretending to drink tea in them. I woke up with his face clouding my vision, and I quickly shook him free. I haven't seen Oliver for two weeks. I think it's best for both of us to have some time apart. Fi's face filled my head, and I smiled at the recent days we shared together. She took me to the dentist a few days ago. I had a crown fitted, so unfortunately Mummy will not be starring as Captain Hook at your next birthday party. I feel like Fi and I are in our teens again, playing at being adults. We've cast aside the worries of the real world and become entirely consumed in dog walking and other simple pleasures. I smiled and headed to the bathroom to wash my face.

Fi's toothbrush sat next to mine in the pot, the two nestled together like penguins in the cold. I waited for the water to warm slightly and I scrutinised my face in the bathroom mirror. My cheeks had grown plumper and my hair looked thicker. The whites of my eyes were cream white instead of bloodshot. The grazes from my fall had healed over, and for the first time in a long time, I looked healthy.

I dipped my hands into the water and lathered them with soap. I washed my face and felt trickles of water chase their brothers down my neck and rest in the pools of my collarbone before continuing their journey down my chest. With soap still covering my face, I pulled the plug and waited for the water to drain before turning the tap to ice cold and rinsing my face. I could hear Fi and the tinkling of cutlery downstairs. The ice-cold water mixed with the smell of coffee woke me up. I grabbed a towel, dried myself off and headed back into the bedroom.

The day felt warm from behind my curtains. Throwing them open, I stood topless in the window looking onto the morning activities in the street. Mrs. Candel, two doors down and across, was already out tending her plants. There was a bright purple mat under her knees, and she wore garden gloves that swamped her otherwise slender fingers. A party of troughs, forks and clippers was at her side. I watched for a while as she fumbled with a rose bush she was prepping for the winter to come, taking each flowerhead in her gloved hands and running her finger along the petals, assessing if it was worth waiting to see if the rose would flower once again or to deadhead it and give it another chance from fresh. She called something out and moments later a sprout of water flew from the side of the house. Her husband quickly appeared and passed her the hose. He brought his hand to her forehead and wiped some dirt away before kissing her. The water from the garden hose drowned the rose bush.

I turned away from the window, feeling guilty for witnessing this intimate moment and scanned my room for something to wear. The chair in the corner of the room, which was usually filled with clothes from the previous week, was empty. I heard the soft hum of the washing machine spinning beneath me. Opening one of the built-in wardrobes that I was so against when I first moved in, I scanned the shelves for something. My eyes settled on my old, stretched nightie, the one I wore during those last few months with you. Fi had folded it into a little square and put it with my T-shirts. I pulled it off the shelf and held it up by the shoulders. I let the material fall down to my knees, holding it at arm's length. It had a cartoon drawing of Roger Rabbit behind bars on the front and Roger's body was misshapen and stretched in odd places where I pulled at it during those restless nights. There were baked bean stains at the top. I chuckled as I remembered trying to rest my plate on you all those months ago. There was a darker stain at the bottom of the nightie, the part that should have rested between my legs, and visions of the morning my waters broke filled my head. I quickly shook the visions free, balled up the nightie and tossed it into the wastepaper basket next to my bed.

The clang, clang, clang of a pot being hit with a spoon rang through the house.

"Breakfast!" Fi's voice yelled, just like our mum used to do. With a smile on my face, I headed downstairs.

Fi had put on a spread, and a pot of coffee sat in the middle of the table accompanied by two of my nicer mugs. She even picked some wild flowers from the garden and put them in a vase next to the mugs, just like we used to do when we were kids. Full plates of scrambled eggs, grilled bacon, baked beans, hash browns, sausages and black pudding greeted my eyes. A few slices of French toast had been buttered and were clinging to the edges of the plate with their middles going soggy from the beans. My stomach growled for what I was about to devour.

"Jesus, Fi. What's the occasion?"

"Do I honestly need an occasion to make my big sister breakfast?"

"Yes," I replied. I squinted at her and pursed my lips as I eased myself into my seat.

Fi started faffing around behind me, moving this and that, before eventually taking her seat opposite me. Something was off. My hands were resting on my cutlery, which still lay on the table.

"What are you waiting for? Eat!" Her forehead had a sheen to it as a few pricks of sweat broke the surface.

"Fiona." I struck Mother's tone with her.

"Barbara." She struck it right back.

"What's all this about?"

"Nothing." Her eyes darted from mine before she over exaggerated a roll of them. "Just eat, will you?"

With my eyes remaining on Fi's, I picked up my cutlery. Fi's eyes remained transfixed on her breakfast. She was sat too upright, and she kept changing how she held her cutlery as if nothing felt comfortable. I raised a selection of bacon, scrambled eggs and beans to my mouth and slowly began to chew. Her eyes darted to mine.

"Sleep well?"

"Mhmm," I replied through a mouthful of food, nodding slowly.

"It's a nice day. I thought we could go for a walk later, if you want?"

"Mhmm," I replied once more. My food was becoming more difficult to chew.

"Joey called..." I stopped chewing and looked at her, but her eyes remained on her food. "He needs me to come home. He says the kids are asking all sorts of questions. Plus, the after-school sitter is about to start exams, so she can't look after the boys anymore. He needs me to come home."

I put my cutlery down, put my elbows on the table and linked my fingers over the top of my plate. I looked at her and swallowed my pride.

"When do you need to go?"

"Tonight," she replied. I nodded. I took a swig of coffee and pushed my chair out from under the table.

"Barbara, you haven't even made a dent in your food. Come on."

"Thanks for breakfast. I appreciate it, I do." I headed for the stairs.

"Barbara, we knew I'd have to go back some time. We can't keep living in this...this fantasy. Life isn't a series of walks and picnics."

"You're right, Fi, it isn't. And please allow me to apologise for inviting you into this *fantasy* world of mine. I'm sorry you got caught up in my life." I slammed the kitchen door. In retrospect, it was a little dramatic, but it felt good at the time. I also stomped up the stairs, probably a little over-dramatic too. But with so many memories coming back from my childhood that morning, slamming doors and stomping upstairs felt appropriate. I went back to my room, pulled my blouse off over my head and threw it on the bed. I pushed my head against the cool glass of the window and looked towards Mrs. Candel's garden. She had beheaded the entire rose bush after all. I guess she thought it best to give the entire plant a chance to give life another go.

A knock at my door brought my attention away from Mrs. Candel's garden and the abandoned hose on her lawn.

"Barbara, can I come in?" I moved over to the door, put my back against it, and slid down to the floor. I heard Fi's knees click as she did the same. I remembered doing the very same thing in your room, Aiden. Fi's breaths were heavy in the silence between us. I wondered if she would slip me another note:

"There's some food in the microwave for you.

Fi."

"We knew I'd have to go back sometime, Barbara. It's not because I love you any less, but I just have..." She couldn't find the words to air her thoughts.

I considered how I would say what she wanted to in my head but couldn't manage it either. I was giving her a hard time.

I sighed. "Fi, honestly it's fine. All this time, I knew this was never going to be permanent. I just wish I could have you a little longer."

"Barbara, I honestly don't think you need me. Think about all we've done together—the walks we've taken and the conversations we've had. You've come a long way since I first arrived. Surely you can tell that you're looking healthier and feeling healthier, right? Plus, you know I'll be back to visit as often as I can. I just have to go now."

I sighed again. She was right. It was always easier for me to swim when I was thrown in the deep end. I feel like Fi has built the most buoyant of life floats I could ask for.

"Now, can we walk Saada, please?" As if on cue, Saada barked from the garden. Fi chuckled from the other side of the door. I could practically hear her smiling.

"Of course we can, My Love."

Up until now, if anyone had been watching our life, they would have seen a direct repeat of a darker time. Except this time, I got up, Fi got up, and the door opened. I hugged her and held her for a good long time before Saada's whining forced us to break our embrace and head downstairs.

We slipped on our boots, put on our coats and pulled our hair back, readying ourselves for battle. The sun shone bright. Saada's tail thump, thump, thumped against my legs. I pulled open the garden gate, and we headed down the street.

"Apparently the boys have been driving Joey up the wall. They're constantly asking when I'll be back, if I was even planning on coming back or if I'd taken a forever holiday like their friend's mum did." Fi looked at me. "They're asking about you, too, Barb. They want to know when they'll get to see their aunty again. It would be great if you could come and visit soon."

"I will. How are they doing at school?"

"Jack seems to be king of his class. He's acing his spelling tests every Friday and has just been made captain of the Rounders team. Fred, on the other hand, isn't doing so well. I think he's feeling lost in his brother's shadow. He'll be ok. He just hasn't quite found his calling yet. You know what I mean? Barbara? What's up?"

I'd stopped in my tracks. Saada, too. Two figures had just turned the corner at the end of the street. Two young boys. One was about a head taller than the other and had a head of thick, brown, curly hair. The shorter of the two had a head of strawberry blonde hair and was just sliding a pair of glasses into his top pocket. *Surely not. What day is it?* I resumed my stride, a lot slower, more cautious.

Saada raised her head high in the air, and her tongue lolled out of her mouth. She sniffed at the breeze and started barking and jumping from side to side. The younger boy, with the shock of strawberry blonde hair, tried to pick up his pace. Oliver's hand fell hard on his shoulder and held him back.

Deep breaths.

I could feel Fi's eyes boring into the side of my head. Then her eyes shot from me to the boys and from the boys back to me. The distance between us closed, painfully slowly, with Saada tugging hard on her lead and me almost leaning backwards trying to counter her strength. The conversation between Fi and I had long been forgotten as she watched the tension unfurl.

Twenty metres.

My eyes locked with Oliver's as I tried to read his expression.

Ten metres.

Saada pulled hard, and I reluctantly let go. She barrelled towards the boys, and Rupert fell to his knees to embrace the welcome. Saada smothered every inch of his face with sloppy kisses, and Rupert laughed trying to hold her steady. Oliver's eyes remained on mine.

"Barbara?" Fi asked something else, but I didn't quite catch it. The sounds of the street had been muffled out.

Five metres.

Rupert and Saada remained where they were, but Oliver kept walking towards me. We all stopped.

I couldn't help but think we were in a scene from a Texas shoot-up. Like cowboys at dawn, we waited for the other to make a move.

Draw.

Fi took a step back. Her questions could wait until later.

"Mum noticed I've been wearing my old school shoes. She's asking where my boots are."

A cold chill swept over me as I remembered Oliver's boot in my bedside cabinet.

"You haven't thrown it out have you, and my coat as well?"

I swallowed and tried to speak. This was ridiculous. A 13-year-old boy had the power to mute a grown woman. I shook my head. Rupert stood up beside a now-calm Saada and was gently patting her side as Fi began talking to him. I strained to hear what they were saying, but Oliver's voice had filled my head, along with something else. Another noise was niggling away at the back of my mind. I couldn't quite make out what it was.

"Well, could I get it all back at some point? If you're heading out now, then maybe Rupert and I can stop by tomorrow after my game?"

I nodded my approval. The noise was getting louder as I allowed myself to look directly at Oliver and become lost in his eyes. He was speaking to me, but I couldn't work out what he was saying. Fi and Rupert had stopped talking, too. Fi was looking at me. Her mouth was moving, but I couldn't hear her either.

The noise at the back of my head grew louder still, like the patter of rain on a tent, coming in short, loud bursts. A storm was coming. Fi was competing with the sound of your rattle. She moved towards me with an arm outstretched. My legs grew weak, and my head felt as light as the clouds you lay on. Fi's voice was completely drowned out. The sound of your music stopped the world from turning.

Everyone stop and listen. Isn't it beautiful?

I woke up with my head on Fi's lap staring up at the sky and her oval face. Worry filled her eyes, and her mouth was moving. The sound of your music had vanished.

"Barbara? Are you okay, Honey?"

"What happened?" I croaked like a frog from a Disney movie.

"You blacked out. You could have really hurt yourself if I hadn't caught you in time." I tried to sit up, but Fi pushed me firmly back down. "Just lay here for a minute, Love."

I looked to my left and saw Saada had taken the liberty of keeping me company. She lay alongside me with her heavy head on her paws, her eyes on mine. She licked my nose.

"How long was I out for? I feel like I've slept forever."

"Not long. You shouldn't have skipped breakfast. You know, Mum used to do the same if she skipped a meal in the morning? You need to look after yourself." She pulled my hair, matted to my face with sweat, away from my eyes. I tried to sit up once again, and this time, Fi helped me to a sitting position.

"Let's take it easy, Barbara, I caught you the first time, but don't push your luck." She smiled at me, and I smiled back. I turned over onto my hands and knees. I pushed myself up. I felt like a foal handling so many limbs for the first time in its life. Fi was at my side with one arm under mine, and the other wrapped around my back.

"I've got it from here, Fi. Thanks."

"You sure?"

"Honestly, I'll be fine."

Cautiously, she let me go, her arms fanned out in the same way our father did when he taught us to ride a bike. He ran behind us, pushing the bike along for a bit before letting go. His arms fanned to his sides and he watched us from a slight squat position. He'd tilt his head from left to right as if that would help us keep our balance as we flew away from him. It took us both months before we plucked enough courage to take a few fingers off the handlebars and learnt to press the brakes. Before we learnt how to use the brakes, we either slowed our pedalling or our father had to sprint after us to catch the bike again. If he didn't make it in time, we simply slowed down enough that our bikes came to a halt. We'd let the bike fall to the side, our hands still gripping the bars and our eyes tightly shut. We had bruises up our arms for weeks.

I looked at her with as much reassurance as I could muster.

"Honestly, Fi, I'm good from here." She backed away a little, but her arms still bobbed out to the side and she was still in a slight squat.

"Where did the boys go?"

"The little one started breathing really heavy, and they didn't have his asthma pump, so they had to take off pretty quickly. They really wanted to stay and help, but I ordered them home. It's enough action for one day having you pass out on me. I can't handle a child's asthma attack, too."

"Oh, poor Rupert."

"That's his name? He said his brother used to help you walk Saada quite a lot."

"He did."

"Now I feel bad because I've stolen some poor boy's pocket money." She winked at me, and I smiled back.

"Did either of them say anything else?"

"I think the older boy said something about tomorrow as they were running off, but I didn't quite catch it. You're already making plans without me?"

"Okay. I think he wants to pick up a few things he left behind." I trailed off.

I smiled again and took Saada's lead from her hands. We continued on our walk and with our small talk. The sun could not set quickly enough.

26th November

Dear Aiden,

Aunty Fi left about half an hour ago. She had her things packed and by the door by the time I got changed after our walk. The house is quiet, really quiet. Even Saada isn't keeping me company. She's been lying by the front door since Fi left, with her tail slowly shifting from side to side and thumping on the linoleum. *Tick-tock.* I don't know what to do with myself. Time is passing so slowly. If I could, I'd go to sleep right now so tomorrow will come around quicker.

Oliver is coming over tomorrow. *Tomorrow!* I decided to clean up, just in case he came inside. Sweet, sweet Oliver. I've missed him, I really have. I got his boot out from my bedside cabinet. I hung his coat back by the front door and I put the boot in the kitchen by the back door. That's a suitable place to keep one lonely boot, isn't it? When he gets here, I'll show him through the house to the back door and point to it and say, "There you go, Mr. Oliver. One school boot just as you left it." He'll thank me, collect his shoe and take his coat from the hooks, and then he'll ask to stay for a drink.

Tomorrow is a big day for both of us. We're going to get our baby back.

Dear Aiden,

Rupert and Oliver came around earlier than I expected today. It must have been around one. Of course, I was ready for them. I had done nothing other than wait that morning. Wait and move Oliver's boot from place to place around the house, searching for its most authentic, temporary home. Finally, they knocked.

"Hi boys. How are you doing? How was the game?" All smiles and hair flicks, like a worker bee in spring.

"Fine. Thanks, Ms. Bridges." Oliver shifted from one foot to the other on the mat. Rupert, just behind him, poked his head out from the side and pushed his glasses up his nose. He was trying to peek past me into the house. I turned a little, satisfying his curiosity.

"Would you like to come in? I'm just about to hose down Saada in the garden. You boys could help, if you like?"

Rupert's eyes lit up, and he tugged at his brother's sleeve. Oliver jerked his arm from his grip.

"We can't stay long, Ms. Bridges. I just need to pick up my coat and boot."

"Of course, of course. Now, where did I put it?" I put on a theatrical show as I rifled through the shoe pile by the door, and then looked in cupboards, and under the stairs. I saw Rupert poking his head further and further around his brother's side. He craned his neck trying to take in as much as he could see. Oliver pushed him back.

"You know, it's a real shame you boys can't hang around for a little while. Saada is one messy pup in the back garden, and I know she'd love to see you both."

The truth is that Saada had been a messy pup since about nine this morning. The poor girl was desperate to be hosed down. The mud was drying and beginning to crack over her fur. She kept pawing at the tap in the back garden. I don't think she was too happy, but we all had parts to play and sacrifices to make.

I drifted into the front room. Your presents were still a little ruffled in the corner. I left the hallway door open and pricked my ears up trying to hear what the two of them were whispering about.

"Please, please, please, Oliver. Pleeeeeeease."

I didn't catch the reply from Oliver, but I could only imagine the look he gave his little brother as the pleading stopped just as briskly as it started. I decided to try one last time. I drifted back into the hallway with my back stiff and my arms placed at my sides.

"I can't find it anywhere, Oliver. Do you want to try and have a look for it yourself? Sorry, I'm so useless sometimes." Sweat pricked on my forehead as Oliver's eyes narrowed on mine, and he did that head tilt that caught my attention all that time ago. We were waiting for the other to make the first move. I didn't shift my weight or break eye contact. I tried to keep my facial expression neutral, daring him to challenge me. My lip began to twitch. Luckily for me, Rupert made the decision for us.

"No one is useless, Ms. Bridges. We'll find it in no time. Don't you worry. Come on, Oliver, let's find it."

He didn't look back at his brother; he just slipped past and took his shoes off before Oliver could object. Oliver's eyes stayed trained on mine as I tried to hide my excitement. Beads of sweat were running down my temples. I pushed them back into my hair as I rearranged my ponytail. Rupert came right up to me.

"Where shall we start looking, Ms. Bridges? Let's retrace our steps. Where did you see it last?"

He sounds just like Audrey.

"I guess the kitchen would be the best place to start?"

"Perfect." Rupert pushed his way past me, and his eyes lit up as he headed into the kitchen. Oliver stepped into the hallway, his eyes dark as moss and still on mine.

"I'll keep my shoes on, if that's okay with you, Ms. Bridges?" He spoke slowly, cautiously.

"That's fine, Love," I sighed and followed Rupert into the kitchen. Of course, he wasn't in there. He had already slid the patio door open and was wrestling Saada to the ground. His socks were caked in mud, and his white fleece was covered in muddy paw prints. I laughed, a genuine laugh.

"Looks like you'll need a hose down too, after this, Rupert!" I called.

"I don't mind! Me and Saada are a team," he shouted back, and Saada yapped her approval.

Oliver joined me at the patio door. He stood by my side with one hand on his hip. I could feel the heat of his body next to mine. I'm not sure if I imagined the hairs of his arms prickling mine, but it gave me goose bumps. I was so aware of how heavy my breathing had become. I wasn't sure if I was breathing too fast, too slow, or too loud.

"You smell like Mum." Oliver said. I panicked and stepped out onto the patio, needing to put some distance between us.

"Rupert, will you help me with the hose?"

Rupert ran over with Saada at his heels, until she realised what was about to happen. Saada turned on the spot and sprinted back into the middle of the garden and braced herself for the onslaught. We unwound the hose from its harness on the wall and turned the tap on, fast. Water plumed out of the end and rocketed into the sky. Overcome with excitement, Rupert grabbed the hose from my hands. His giggles danced through the garden like butterflies. He pushed his thumb and forefinger down on the end of the hose, and the water fanned out. It caught the light and created a rainbow of every colour for Saada to jump through. Out of the corner of my eye, I saw Oliver disappear back into the house. I followed him inside, leaving Rupert and Saada to play under a rainbow of naivety. I found him in the front room staring at your presents.

"How's the hunt going?" I asked. I leaned against the wall with my arms crossed, trying to be as small as I could.

He raised Rupert's football boot and his own school boot, one in each hand. A small smile swept over his face. His eyes were full of something new. I nodded, acknowledging the elephant in the room.

Oliver turned his face to mine. "What happened to you, Ms. Bridges?" he asked. I sighed. Where do I even begin with a question like that? "Did you get sick?"

"Sort of, I guess." I crossed my arms a little tighter. Silence fell between us for a moment while I mulled over how to approach this situation. How was I to air what had happened to us without being swept into the tornado of emotions that usually accompanies thoughts of you, Aiden?

"I lost my baby."

"You lost it?" Oliver's head cocked to one side.

I walked further into the front room and perched on the arm of the sofa. Oliver tracked my every move. He ran the laces of his brother's boot between his fingers.

"*He* is called Aiden, but unfortunately he was born with a heart of gold. He was born so rich in love that the angels decided to take him. They wanted to share him with the rest of the world." My sentences were punctured with sharp breaths, like needles piercing balloons at the end of a party.

"So, where is he now?"

"You know, I ask myself the same question every day." He put down his belongings on top of one of your presents and walked up to me. A hand fell heavily on my shoulder. A slow, awkward pat followed. I kept my eyes to the ground.

"We lost our grandpa last year. It was the first time I've ever lost anything since my goldfish died when I was seven."

There it was Aiden—your rattle, tinkling away in the background as you'd been placed in the same category as death. You were not dead. You could not be dead. You were simply elsewhere.

"I didn't really understand what had happened to Grandpa until Mum explained it to me properly. It's so sad to think that I won't see him again, but that doesn't mean he can't see me. I know he sees me and Rupert every day. I know he protects us, and Mum told me to be happy for the life he had."

It was a perfect example of how wise this young boy is, wise beyond his years. I looked up at him and caught a glimpse of the man he would become. There was a depth in his eyes I'd never noticed before. He'll become the type of man I could fall in love with, fall into life with.

His hand burnt through my top, and my shoulder was on fire. He squeezed, and I stood up. I broke away from those green fields in his eyes. We will have picnics and fly kites in those fields one day, Aiden.

"Ms. Bridges! Saada's brought mud in the house..." Rupert came bounding around the corner and skidded to a stop in the doorway. He held his breath with pursed lips, his eyes darting between us. He was covered head to toe in splotches of mud. Half an oak leaf was caught in his hair, and there was a streak of mud on the floor behind him. He held the doorframe, looked at his hands and realised he got mud on the frame. His eyes flitted between the mud stain and us as he tried to wipe it off as discreetly as possible.

"What are you guys talking about?" he asked.

Oliver looked at me before looking back to his brother. Rupert began chewing his tongue in concentration as his fingers rubbed the mud into the paintwork. Oliver looked back at me and gestured his head towards his muddy brother. There he was, a child again, exchanging secrets in the playground. I nodded my approval and sighed. I looked past Oliver and out through the slats in the shutters. Even if my body was here, I could try to take my mind elsewhere. I wasn't sure if I could handle the fact that he was about to talk about you.

"Ms. Bridges had a baby, Rupert."

"No way! Really? Where is he? Or she? Although I think I'd prefer..."

Oliver's hand shot out, palm flat towards his brother. Rupert pursed his lips again, clearly confused but accepting that it was not the time to speak.

"*He* is called Aiden," Oliver said. Rupert's eyes lit up. "And he is with Grandpa now."

Rupert froze with his mouth open like he was about to speak. He closed it with a puzzled look on his face.

"Grandpa...on Mummy's side?"

Oliver nodded. Rupert hung his head and let his hand drop from the doorframe. I could practically hear the cogs whirring away behind those beautiful eyes.

"So...so does that mean..."

I brought my focus back from outside and looked at Oliver's grave face. He nodded once more. I felt my eyes pushing salty water and felt drops begin to burst out of hiding. A drop hit my hand, and I felt like it chimed through the room.

"We should really go, Ms. Bridges." Oliver's heavy hand gave me two awkward pats before he grabbed his things and moved towards his brother.

My eyes stayed on the teardrop on top of my hand. I could make out stressed whispering in the hall but couldn't quite hear what the two were bickering about. I can't say I tried. I wanted to hear your rattle. I needed to hear that and only that. I needed to know you could see me as well as Grandpa Harp could see his boys. The front door creaked, and a gentle thud let me know the two boys had left.

I eased myself away from the wall and took a breath. Listening for your rattle, I headed out of the front room and heard that soft tinkering. It pulled me into the kitchen. Saada was still rolling around in the mud outside, and there you were. Your little muddy prints covered my kitchen floor. Your rattle screamed from the cabinets, the sink, and the oven. It screamed with such determination that it brought me to my knees right in front of your footprints, which had run their path towards and over my heart. I crawled towards one in particular, one in which I could make out each of your little toes, and I laid alongside it with my head on my arm.

This little piggy went to market. I traced my finger over your big toe.

This little piggy stayed home. My eyes grew heavy as your rattle shook the walls so hard that the tiles started to fall and smash on the work surfaces.

This little piggy had roast beef. It rained ceramics around me, and your cry grew louder.

This little piggy had none. Your eyes were field green, and there were freckles across your nose. Your hair was strawberry blonde.

This little piggy went all the way home.

29th November

Dear Aiden,

I can't do it. I can't bring myself to wipe up your footsteps. I can't bring myself to wipe away your smudged prints off the front room doorframe. Not now. Not ever. Each little piece that you've left behind is so perfect. It's exactly what I imagined you would be. Instead, I'll walk the same path as you each morning. Not Oliver's path. He's too old for our games. I'll walk the same path as you, Rupert. I'll make you lunch. I'll look after you. I'll ensure those little steps of yours grow and turn into great strides with me at your side.

Dear Aiden,

Weeks have trickled into months. A new world has been created. A world that is ours and that no one else can hinder or harm. Now that you're old enough to walk to school on your own, life is easier for us. I've grown used to the smell of your strawberry blonde hair and have learnt to carry a spare asthma pump in my pocket. We are not perfect, but we are close to it. Maybe I should prepare your room?

I remember painting your nursery in those early months. I got a touch of paint and put a spot of it on my nose before going to look at myself in the bathroom mirror. I looked like a practical mum. I looked great. My hair was a mess. I chose an old pair of dungarees to paint in, my nail varnish was flaking off, and I was glowing. I had this lovely little bump in my belly and a paintbrush in my hand.

For all the worrying I did about how to be a mother, I did equal amounts of worrying on how to look like a mother. I wanted to look like I was taking all of it in my stride. I wanted to look like my pregnancy was all in a day's work and not nine agonising months. I bought oversized cardigans and safe sandals. I bought earthy-coloured tops that complemented large, gold jewellery. I drank homemade smoothies and took vitamins I didn't know existed. I was going to look the part as much as I possibly could.

The day I started to decorate your nursery, I truly looked the part. And in the end, I felt the part. I was a mother.

I am a mother.

I looked at myself in the mirror and brushed a few more streaks of paint across my face and arms. I couldn't stop smiling. I wanted someone to knock at the door so I could open it looking like that and get all flustered and say, "Sorry, I wasn't expecting visitors."

I called Aunty Fi, but she wasn't answering. I needed someone to see me. So I cleaned out everything I could find and managed to fill a trash bag. I took one last look at myself in the hallway mirror. I pulled a few more strands of hair out from my ponytail and practised blowing them out of my face. Then, barefoot, I headed out to the front garden with one hand on bump, and the other carrying an exceptionally light trash bag.

Someone see me.

Mrs. Dewley from the corner happened to be passing by. She was walking her cat, which is something I never understood. But ,she seemed adamant that her old puss would lose its way if she let her out of the house on her own. The cat didn't seem to mind. I always wondered who was walking whom. Mrs. Dewley had the type of posture that made me straighten my back. She still had a head full of thick hair, which always amazed me considering her age. I imagine she's one of the few women who still sleep in curlers.

She was wearing a mustard yellow dress with pink flowers all over it. It brushed along her ankles. Mrs. Dewley takes great pride in her appearance. She always has a face full of makeup. Her nails are always painted the same pearly pink, and I've never seen her wear the same piece of jewellery twice, save for her wedding ring.

As far as I know, her husband passed away a few years before I moved onto the street. From what the other neighbours tell me, it took her an entire year before she was able to leave the house again. I couldn't imagine a grief like that, spending so many years with someone you love, and then one day they are just gone, and you are left with nothing but memories. Then, as you get older, you don't even have those.

Mrs. Dewley had been nothing but kind to me since I arrived on the street. She was always offering her help around the house, even though she would be more of a hindrance than anything else. She invited me in for tea more times than I can remember. I was counting on her at this exact moment to offer her help. To look up and compliment me on how glowing I was. Thank you, Mrs. Dewley, thank you for leaving those rose-netted curtains behind on that particular day. Thank you for walking past my house and for pulling through for me.

"Hello, Missy. I see you're having a productive day." She winked at me.

"Why hello, Mrs. Dewley. I am indeed. Thanks for noticing."

I blew a strand of hair out of my face. "I think I've managed to get more paint over myself than I have over this little one's nursery." I gave you an affectionate pat, and you kicked back.

"Well, it's very becoming on you, Dear."

I beamed back at her. "Thank you, Mrs. Dewley."

"Well, I'll get back to it then. No rest for the wicked, right?" I gave her a cheeky grin, and she chuckled back at me.

"Have a nice day. Send my love to the little one." She nodded towards my belly, towards you.

Thank you, Mrs. Dewley. You have no clue what that meant to me. You made me feel like a mother.

3rd July

Dear Aiden,

Your birthday is on its way, and Mummy has picked you out some beautiful, beautiful presents. You're going to have the most incredible day. A day you deserve. After everything we have been through, after everything we've seen and done together, we deserve a good day. The world owes it to us. Now Mummy just needs to find wrapping paper to match. Mummy needs to find one your friends won't laugh at. Kids can be so cruel sometimes. Don't worry. It's just part of growing up.

I remember when I was in school. I couldn't have been more than 13. There was a boy a few years above me. He was a big boy, big-boned with broad shoulders and a huge meaty head. He had dark blue eyes that looked like the Cornish Sea in a storm, and a mop of dirty blonde hair that curled into waves with the wind. I always had the bad luck of my classes being in the same building as his. And no matter where I chose to spend my lunch break, he was always there. He made my high school experience terrifying.

The school grounds were huge; at least they seemed huge to me at the time. I would come home from school, take off my leather shoes, and my mother would rub salts into my heels while we sat on the sofa. I'd tell her about the woes of my day, how far I'd had to walk, and the stairs I'd had to climb.

On my first day of school, I sprinted to my French class. I'd heard a lot about the teacher and how strict she was. I liked French, and I didn't want to start by making a bad impression. But I got lost en route, and I ended up in the science block instead of languages with only minutes to spare. I sprinted around the library and straight into this hunk of a man. That's what he seemed like to me, Aiden—a man in a child's school uniform. I accidentally knocked a portion of chips and gravy out of his hands and down the front of his shirt.

"Watch it, Lesbo," he spat at me. I'd never been called a lesbian before. Heck, I didn't even really know what a lesbian was, but I remember thinking that it couldn't be a good thing. He grieved for his chips before he looked up at me with all the rage of the Cornish coastline, his eyes shimmering like marbles.

"Why have you got hair like a boy? Do you *want* to be a boy?" his friends began to chip in. Your nana had cut my hair just days before, Aiden. She said it looked smart.

"I only figured she was a girl because of the earrings," another one of his friends piped up.

"Dilan, you've got bigger boobs than her!" They were surrounding me.

"You owe me a portion of chips, Lesbo," the huge boy told me. He scraped the gravy off his shirt and slapped it across my face. The boys left in a flurry of laughter as the second bell rang. I stood outside the library, covered in gravy, humiliated and late for class. I went to the toilets and sat in a cubicle for the whole of French. At lunch, I went home. When my mother got back from work and asked how school was, I replied, "Fine."

From that day, Dilan went out of his way to make my life that little bit harder. In the autumn, he'd fling mud at me. In the summer months, he'd throw up my skirt and ask if there was anything under there. Every time, I went to the same cubicle in the library toilets—the ones no one used—and I sat out my next class. Taking deep breaths, I went to the bathroom mirror and dissected myself. He called me ugly. He told me no one liked me. He told me I looked like a lesbian. So I went to the bathroom mirror and told myself repeatedly, "You are beautiful. People like you. You are not a lesbian." But, by the time I was halfway through high school, these names had been thrown at me so often by him and his friends that I started to believe them.

One early spring, we had a heat wave, and I wore tights to school. I remember wanting to cover myself up as much as possible back then. I was self-conscious and naïve to the changes happening to my body. I must have been 15 or so. My school blazer was over my arm and I was fanning myself with one of my textbooks. Normally, I would stick to the main roads on my walk home. But that day, I cut through the alley because it was quicker. The alley was in the shade, and I could feel a breeze running through it as quick as a river.

"Well, if it isn't our little lesbian friend!"

"Look at her with her tits out."

"At least, she's got tits, now. You're not half bad, you know that, Lesbo?"

I looked down at my blouse. I'd undone a few buttons for the hot walk home. The boys had sought refuge by the back exit of a kebab store. Bits of tomato and limp lettuce littered the ground around them.

"Why you got those legs covered up, Lesbo? There something you're hiding from us?"

"Maybe we should make sure she's definitely a girl?"

"She's a girl, look at her tits! You ever heard of a bra, Lesbo?"

I'd been meaning to ask my mother for a bra for the last couple of weeks. My body was changing, and I was humiliated by it. My legs were prickly, my breasts hurt all the time, and my nipples were showing through my blouse. Earlier that week, I woke up to bloody sheets and went to my mother in tears. I was so scared she would be angry with me, but instead she just hugged me. I wanted nothing more than for my mother to hug me at that moment.

The boys placed their half-eaten kebabs on top of a dumpster and blocked my path. A couple slipped behind me to stop me from running back to the main street.

"Let's see what she's hiding." One of the boys grabbed my blouse and tore it open.

"Maybe yours are bigger after all, Dilan," he laughed.

I looked down at my swollen breasts; one was slightly bigger than the other. I never felt so ashamed. One of the boys came up behind me and lifted my skirt while the other tore down my tights. I remember the ladder screeching its way down to my ankles as he pulled.

"You scream, and I'll kill you," Dilan said.

I put my own hand over my mouth, and the tears came flooding down. He grabbed my crotch. His hand felt hot as an iron on my skin.

"She's bleeding! She's fucking bleeding. Fuck, it's on my hand. It's on my hand! That is so fucking gross!"

The toilet paper I'd lined my underwear with had slipped, and I could feel blood trickling down my legs. He pulled his hand away from me, but my blood was running down his wrist already. He gagged. He shoved me to the side. I fell and hit my head on the dumpster. The boys ran off down the alleyway screaming with laughter at their friend. I laid on the ground for a minute discarded like the vegetables around me.

No one had ever touched me there before. No one was ever supposed to. I felt like I'd done a bad thing because I let them. I was so ashamed that I let them. I pulled my tights back up. The ladder tore its way up to my crotch. I put my blazer on and buttoned it up over my blouse. I went home, sweating, crying and riddled with mayonnaise and guilt.

My mum had got home early that day, and I couldn't bear to look at her as I walked through the front door.

"What happened to your tights, Baby?"

Fresh tears poured from my eyes, and I sprinted up to my room and slammed the door behind me. As I pulled off my tights, they cracked against the dried blood on my legs and pulled at stray hairs. A few moments later my mother let herself in and sat next to me on the bed. She put her arm around me and held me to her. She smelt of Dove soap.

"Mum, am I ugly?"

"You are beautiful."

"Do you think people like me?"

"Why wouldn't they, Dear? You're the kindest person I know."

"Mum, what if I'm a lesbian?"

My mother was silent. She got up and left the room. I cried even harder. She came back a few moments later with a bag. I looked at her. I was so sorry, and I wasn't sure why.

"I got you these today." She pulled out a pack of sanitary pads and a few peach-coloured bras. She put them on my desk. She came over to me, knelt in front of me, and put both her hands on my shoulders. "Look at me."

I looked up, and then looked away immediately. I couldn't take the humiliation.

"Barbara Bridges, look at me," she persisted. "You are kind, you are beautiful, and you are my daughter. I will love you no matter what."

She brought me into her arms, and I cried my guilt into her shoulders. "I'll put the bath on for you," she whispered.

Kids can be so cruel.

One month to go.

Dear Aiden,

I mixed up your usual packed lunch for today. I hope you like it. Don't let anyone else see it, though, I don't want them getting jealous. There are a few treats in there I'm not sure the teachers will be too happy about. Perhaps it's a little too much sugar, but as long as we make sure you brush your teeth every morning and night, you'll be fine.

Your presents are wrapped, and I found a cake recipe. I can't believe how much sugar they put into these things too. You'll be up for days. I'll feel bad sending your friends home at the end of it all. Their parents will never forgive me. The cake is going to be spectacular, though. I've never really baked much before, but I've adopted habits in my life that I presume a mother should have, baking being one of them.

No matter how prepared you think you are to be a mother, it's never really enough. Those nine months fly by, and suddenly there's a baby in your arms. It dawns on you that you actually know nothing about being a mother. I read parenting books and watched videos online, but the nearest thing to practice was playing with dolls when I was a few years older than you would be now.

I used to have a doll called Lilly. She was a glorious little thing with hay yellow hair and buttons for eyes. She had a permanent grin on her face, and her hand squeaked when you pressed it. Mother washed her after a trip through the forest one weekend, and she stopped squeaking. I didn't mind though, because she smelt of lavender. I used to sleep with her at night, resting her face on the pillow alongside me to ensure the duvet wouldn't stifle her breaths. I had a little tub of plastic baby food that smelt like cherries, and I fed her before I ate my own dinner every night.

Caring for Lilly came so naturally to me. It was her first and her always. She fit into my arms so snugly, and I rocked her to sleep on long car journeys. I whispered secrets in her ears when my parents weren't around. I cut her hair enough times that she could no longer manage hairstyles. My mother kept asking if I wanted a new one, as if Lilly were simply disposable. How could I ever exchange my Lilly? You're stuck with the child you get, and you love the child you get no matter what happens to them or what they look like. No one was going to take Lilly away from me, even if she didn't squeak anymore. No other doll could replace her.

One day, I got home from school and Lilly was gone, along with the few teddies I owned. I ran into Fi's room, and all of hers were gone as well.

"Where are they?" I panicked, and Fi shook her head, bewildered as she crawled out from under her bed. Her eyes were watery, and her bottom lip was quivering like a loose, autumn leaf in the wind. Our mother stormed into the room with a pair of kitchen scissors in her hand.

"Girls, I'm so sorry," she said. "Follow me."

We followed her into the driveway. A few black bin bags were waiting to be picked up by tomorrow's garbage men. She took the pair of scissors and raised them high above her head. I remember them catching the light of the sun and blinding me for a second. When I could see again, she'd brought the scissors down and slashed into the first bin bag. A bundle of colour flooded out. Our dolls.

"Your father had a clear out. I can't believe he did this. Take what you want and hide it, okay?" We nodded vigorously at our mother, so thankful she was on our side. Lilly's non-squeaky hand reached out towards me. I snatched her up and ran inside the house. I stroked what was left of her hair and promised her I would never let anything bad happen to her again.

I tried for years to have you, Aiden. So many years filled with so much hope. I was beginning to think you would never arrive. I felt I'd failed as a woman. The same waves of guilt rushed over me as that day I ran home from school with the buttons of my blouse left scattered across the alleyway.

When I found out I was pregnant with you, I almost passed out. I had so many pregnancy tests show up negative that I honestly thought that one would be the same. I barely even looked at it. I was standing over the bin, ready to drop it in when I saw the second line appear. The first image that came to mind was Lilly. My mind raced back to the night I held her in my arms and promised that I would never let anything bad happen to her. Lilly's face became fleshed out and more rounded in my mind. Her button eyes were overcome with storm-cloud marble eyes that some babies have in their first few weeks. Her rag doll body plumped out and became human flesh. She suddenly looked huge in my childlike arms.

I remember wondering how I would even hold you. What if you squirmed? What if you couldn't fall asleep on my breasts and everything just felt uncomfortable? What if you didn't have that newborn baby smell that so many mothers talk about? What would I cook for you? How much would I cook for you? How long was I supposed to feed you from my breast? How would I get you to sleep at night? How long should I let you sleep? What music should I play to you? When should I start reading to you? What if I don't fall instantly in love with you? There were so many questions, so many doubts. Not for one second did I ever think, *What if you don't arrive?*

24 days to go.

Dear Aiden,

Themes are a tricky thing. Anything too difficult and people would rather not show up. Anything too easy and people won't really bother. You have to settle on something smart, something that people will read, smile approvingly and think, "Yeah, that's a good one." I've been to a few themed parties in my time and some were incredible; others, not so much. I've attended three themed parties that really stood out for me. *Alice in Wonderland*, *Fast Food* and *Under the Sea*.

Alice in Wonderland was the most memorable. The birthday girl was an old friend from school and, surprisingly, her name was Alice. She was a little blonde thing, filled with hope and ambition. She wanted to open a gallery, move south and live happily ever after. I'm not sure what she's doing now. I know she married well. Maybe she doesn't need to run a gallery and just paints for the fun of it. Anyway, the party was small, 14 or so of us. She assigned us each a role from the book that best fit our personality. Her boyfriend at the time was assigned the Cheshire Cat. My flatmate got the Mad Hatter, and I got the White Rabbit. I took the hint—my time management was poor. However, I made the most out of my character and turned up two hours late. I was planning on one hour, but as I said, time management.

Luckily, everyone thought it hilarious and as soon as I arrived to complete the cast, the night was set.

She decorated her apartment in oversized things. We drank cocktails from teacups, and there were cupcakes labelled: *Don't eat me*. Everything was exquisite. It was the perfect example of a successful theme.

The *Fast Food* party was organised by someone on my university campus. People got really into it, and word quickly got out that there would be a lot of paper mâché involved. We were students—kings and queens of procrastination. Of course, we gallantly sacrificed lectures and deadlines in order to prepare for the party of the semester, even though we had about a month's notice. I have never known such a large group of students to finish a project with such timely diligence.

We all lived on campus within a five-minute walk from each other, so we regularly checked in on how our works of art were progressing. It was a support group, of sorts. One boy managed to get his hands on the cutout clown from a local McDonalds. However, Mr. McDonald was sacrificed to the volleyball team, which dressed him in their opponent's colours and tore his head off as an intimidation tactic at the start of the league final. *Fast Food* night eventually came around, and of course, it was a Friday. We started the night at the flat where most of our friends lived, and then we headed to town. The theme was successful because of the sheer amount of effort people put in. Honestly, I didn't know half my friends had a creative bone in them. I was studying with lawyers, physiologists, researchers, yet here they were as hamburgers, hot dogs and mustard bottles.

When we arrived in town, we assembled ourselves outside various fast food restaurants and acted out little scenes. We made the local paper as proof that students could be productive when it suited them.

The last successful theme I remember is *Under the Sea*. Again, this was a university event. The secret to this theme was having a prize for the best dressed. The event was hosted by the fine art students to raise money for their exhibition space. They offered face painting at the door in exchange for a contribution towards their space, and the students came through by the hundreds. Entire classes planned themes within the theme. I had to hand it to the marine biologists, who came as the Great Barrier Reef. I'd never seen so many different colours of coral in my life. We can learn two things from this theme, Aiden.

1. An incentive always gets the competition going.
2. Everyone loves face paint.

I'm remembering this as I plan your party. How do we choose a theme for you, Mister? I want to steer away from anything that would be dated—no current celebrities, current affairs or cartoon characters. I don't want to look back at the photos and think, "Why did we do that? Who was she supposed to be?"

I want to create some competition. I'm thinking Career Day. What do you think? It would be amazing to have little firemen and astronauts running around the back garden. I like it already. Now all we need to do is find you a white coat that won't trail along the ground, one that will make the ladies swoon as you breeze by.

19 days to go.

24th July

Dear Aiden,

It's all coming together relatively well. I found the decorations. Nothing cheap and cheerful here. I've gone for minimalistic, but they are still elegant and still appropriate for a 9-year-old's birthday party.

I cleaned the house from top to bottom, and I have banned Saada from certain rooms until your big day. I don't need to keep going over the sofa with a sticky roller. She's moulting like there's no tomorrow, and I'm not having the only thing people take away from your birthday party being a shirt covered in dog hair. I can't wait to have you back in our home. I can't wait to run my hands through your hair like I used to do with Lilly. I can't wait until you fall asleep in my arms. I can't wait to pinch that freckled nose in the mornings and kiss your forehead before you go to school.

I think I'm ready way ahead of time. Maybe I'll take Saada out this afternoon to get some fresh air on my face. There's only so many times I can reposition the furniture.

10 days to go.

29th July

Dear Aiden,

I see Audrey has bought you a lunch box. Did you not like mine? I doubt she pours as much love into hers. I called out for you on your way home from school today. Maybe you didn't hear me? I just wanted to check in on you and see how your day went. I want to take you to the secret spot I used to go with your brother before he outgrew me. You'll like it there; it's quiet. There will be no one to disturb us.

I hope you hear me tomorrow, Love. You know I can't get too close to the other mums after everything that's happened. Perhaps I'll try waiting for you in a quieter spot tomorrow.

Shall I invite the neighbours? I've heard Mrs. Candel can put together a mean lemon cheesecake.

5 days to go.

Dear Rupert,

You seemed off today. I'll admit, I thought you'd be a little happier to see me.

"Hello, Trouble. How are you?" I called as you turned the corner to where I was waiting. Was it me or did you hesitate just a fraction?

"Hello, Ms. Bridges." You pushed those big glasses of yours back up higher on your nose.

"No need to be so formal with me, Rupert. I know what you're like!" I grinned at you but got nothing back. Perhaps you just had a long day.

"Here." I offered out Saada's lead, and you eventually took it. We began walking together.

"You're quiet. Is there something on your mind?" I asked. You just shook your head and your eyes were trained on the ground ahead of us.

"Well, if you don't feel like talking, then I've got something to say." You looked up at me. You are everything I wanted you to be. "It's a big day for you this week. I've got everything ready."

"A big day?" you asked.

"Your birthday, silly."

"But, my birth..."

"I made a huge cake and bought lots of decorations for the party on the weekend. Have you invited anyone from school yet? I'll probably need to speak to their mothers first. We need to check to make sure no one has any food allergies."

"But, Ms. Bridges..."

"Yes, don't worry. I got you what you've always wanted." I winked down at you. You looked at me, shocked for a moment. Perhaps you couldn't believe that I could possibly know what you've always wanted. Believe you me, I've got it. I grinned at you, and a second later there was that huge grin that I haven't seen in so long. "And I want to cook you your favourite meal."

"Spaghetti bolognese?"

"Whatever you want, Sweetheart. It's your day, not mine."

There was finally a skip in your step as we got to the start of Arweneck Avenue.

"This has to be our little secret for tomorrow, okay? Otherwise I can't give you your present."

"Sure thing." You nodded your head, shaking your glasses loose down your nose again.

"See you tomorrow." I leaned over and kissed you on the forehead. I left you smiling and bewildered on the corner of Arweneck Avenue. I bet you're trying to figure out what surprises I've got in store.

Dear Rupert,

You've done nothing but sulk since we got home. I don't know what's got into you, but it's not wise to be so disobedient just before your birthday. Perhaps it's the change of coming back to my place? I think it's healthy for you to spend some more time with Saada. She misses you. So why all the tears now on the night before your birthday? Don't you want to wake up beside all your presents? Calm down, Love. Stop those tears. Dinner will be ready soon. I'm cooking spaghetti bolognese. Actually, I need to check on that.

———————⊥———————
˙˙˙

"Rupert, come down for your dinner!" Sobs echoed through the hallway. I heard a crash. I climbed the stairs with the hairs on the back of my neck standing on end. I hoped you hadn't damaged anything. I hoped you hadn't hurt yourself. There was silence for the first time since you came home from school. I didn't know what was more worrying, the tears or the silence.

"Rupert? Is everything okay in there?" I knocked gently on the door but still got no reply. Nine going on nineteen already.

"Rupert? I'm coming in." I opened the door and it hit something, giving me only an inch or so before I really had to push.

"Rupert, move out of the way and let Mummy in, please." Polite but firm. I needed to establish who was in charge. I pushed a little harder and realised that it wasn't a 9-year-old resisting. I pushed the door just enough to squeeze my head through. You managed to drag the cot in front of the door. It's a heavy cot. That took dedication.

I pushed a little harder and squeezed my body through the gap. I stayed behind the cot, and there you were, curled in a ball in the corner of the room, your shoulders slowly rising and falling. Perhaps you fell asleep. Perhaps you were trying to calm yourself down. The lamp with the clouds on it fell off the chest of drawers. Its cable was caught underneath one of the legs of the cot. There was glass on the floor from the supposedly shatter-proof bulb. I panicked and scanned the room for blood.

"Aiden, what have you done? There's glass everywhere."

"I don't care," you mumbled into your arms.

"Aiden, come on. What's got into you?"

You mumbled something that I couldn't make out. I looked around the room; it had been so long since I last went in there. The paint had faded a little, perhaps from so many mornings bleaching in the sun. I moved out from behind the cot and ran my hands along the walls. Some flecks from your broken bear still speckled the walls, but most of it had fallen to the floor and flaky patches of grey were left on what used to be white clouds.

"No more tears now, My Love. That's enough, it's just wasted water." I found myself using the same words my mother used to use on me. The same words that I grew to hate. You mumbled something to me.

"What was that?" I asked.

"I want to go home." You shook your head into your arms, fists clenched into tiny little balls no bigger than knots of dough.

"Don't be silly. This is your home, now. With me."

"I want to go HOME!" I took a step back, shocked. I had never heard you shout before.

"What about Saada? Don't you think Saada will be sad?"

You took a deep breath and opened your mouth, only to close it again. Your brow furrowed as fresh tears rimmed the edge of your eyes, and you buried your face in your arms again.

A new mumble.

"What was that?"

You held your head up and looked directly at me. "I don't care about Saada."

"You don't mean that, Aiden. I'll leave you to think about what you said."

I stepped out of the door and gently pulled it closed.

"My name is Rupert!" you screamed, and fresh sobs filled the hallway.

I went downstairs. The spaghetti had boiled over, and there was water all over the hob.

2nd August

Dear Rupert,

It's later now, and two plates of cold and over-cooked spaghetti bolognese are sitting on the table. You are still refusing to come down for tea. You've pushed the cot in front of the door again, and I refuse to force my way back into your bedroom. You'll get hungry enough, eventually. You won't be able to stay up there all night. You'll come down all bleary eyed and filled with apologies. I'll take you into my arms and whisper that everything will be okay. I'll remind you that you shouldn't be wasting water on salty tears.

We'll sit down at the table, and this horrible afternoon will be put behind us. Things can only get easier from here on in. Besides, we have something worth celebrating tomorrow. I decided against inviting the neighbours to your party. I don't even feel like decorating the house at the moment. Your presents are hidden away in my wardrobe, and there they will stay until you start showing me a little more respect. You'll come around. It's all part of growing up.

The doorbell chimes through the house. I'm pulled from my daydream and cautiously step into the hallway. I pause for a moment—silent—listening to see if you've heard the chime from your fort. The floorboards are quiet. I wait a little longer just to double check. The bell chimes again.

Angry, I open the door, perhaps a little too hastily. I am ready to give hell to whoever is disturbing our dinner. I am confused for a moment. My eyes are cast slightly up, expecting to see a salesman or someone from our local council checking to make sure I'd be voting for the right party.

I was greeted with a head of dark curls poking out from a red-check hat. Looking down, Oliver's green, inquisitive eyes greet mine. His face is lit from the orange streetlight on one side and the other half is cast in shadow. I pulled the door closer still. My hand is on my hip. I feel myself grinding my teeth. I can't have you being taken away from me again. Not this time. I shake my head a little and try to shake away my defensive front. I force a smile.

"Oliver, what a lovely surprise. To what do I owe the pleasure?"

"Hi, Ms. Bridges. Can I come in?" His neck cranes, and he tries to look past me.

Good luck, kiddo.

"Now is not really a good time. I close the door a little further. I know he can't see past my body, but I need this conversation to end as soon as possible. What if you hear his voice? What if you call out? Oliver puts his hand on the front door as I try to back away and close it. I'm surprised by his strength. He looks at me with something new in his eyes. A determination I haven't seen before...something almost menacing. He looked like someone I wouldn't want to cross if he had another decade behind him.

"Ms. Bridges, please. I would really like to come in." Polite but firm, I know this tactic.

I got another glance at the man he would one day become. Yet, this time I was not in love with the man he will become, I feared him. I look down, I can visibly see my hand shaking and realise the amount of pressure we are both applying to the door, just to keep it where it is. I sighed. I knew he wasn't going to give up any time soon. The last thing I needed was anyone else asking questions. I don't need any more eyebrows to be raised in my direction. I ease the pressure off the front door and let a child force his way into my house. *I'll continue to act the innocent though. It's not going to get any easier for you, Dear.*

"You'll have to keep your voice down though. Saada is sleeping."

Thank goodness that much is true. Saada laid sprawled across the hallway with her tongue lolling out the front of her mouth and her legs giving the occasional kick. For a moment, I envy her. Things are so much simpler on four legs. Oliver nods his acknowledgement and heads into the kitchen. Good, we're less likely to be heard, and to hear, in here. He turns to face me. I don't think he's thought this far ahead.

"Rupert didn't come home from school today, Ms. Bridges."

I say nothing. I just look at him. I'll let him play his next card first and see what he has in store.

"He didn't come home, and we don't know where he is," he says.

I'm still not entirely sure what to say, or even how to act. My palms are clammy. I wipe them on my jeans, and Oliver notices.

"Have you spoken with the school? Did anyone see him leave?" I ask.

"Mum and Dad don't want to make a fuss just yet. They think he's probably just gone straight to a friend's. It wouldn't have been the first time."

Can he hear my heart? It's pounding so loud it's deafening.

"I just thought I'd stop by. I know he really likes you, Ms. Bridges. Maybe you saw him over the last couple of weeks? Maybe you have an idea of where he could be?"

"I haven't seen him so often, Oliver. I just bump into him sometimes on my walk with Saada. Sometimes, he'll join us if we're going in the direction of your school."

"You're always going in the direction of my school, Ms. Bridges."

Guilty as charged.

"I also know you don't just bump into him. Last week, Mum forgot to give me my lunch money..."

Oh, no.

"I asked Rupert, in the playground, if he had any and he gave me a packed lunch. Mum doesn't give us chocolate for lunch, Ms. Bridges."

I look at my toes. *Did you know my middle toe is bigger than my second? Fun fact.*

"Rupert told me that you've been making him packed lunches just like you used to do for me. He didn't want to say anything because he didn't want to upset Mum. He said you make them better."

I couldn't help but smile at that. I push my chin to my chest and hope that Oliver didn't notice.

"Now, do you understand why I thought I'd come 'round?"

I nod my head, and my hands knot together at my front. I need to get him out. I need this to wrap up. I'm not going to be able to hide my baby for too much longer.

"He told me you were planning a party for him."

"I was. I still am," I mumble into my chest.

"I told him to ignore you."

So that explains his hesitancy.

"Have you seen him, Ms. Bridges? Did he tell you where he was going today?"

I shake my head. I can't trust myself to speak. Oliver is nodding, slowly. There's nothing more he can say if I give him nothing to work with. He sighs.

"I'm sure he'll turn up. There's nothing to worry about, Oliver. Boys will be boys. You should know that." I force a chuckle as I head back into the hall hoping he'll take the hint and follow my lead. I wait by the door. *One, two, three, four...*I don't hear him move. I open the front door. Surely, he's heard that?

Why isn't he coming?

"Ms. Bridges?" He calls from the kitchen.

I stiffen. My eyes darting up the stairs, hoping you haven't heard. I'm not sure what I should do. I really can't afford for him to be in the house much longer. Our luck is wearing thin as a blade of grass. I head back into the kitchen before Oliver decides to call out again. His back is turned to me, and he is facing the kitchen table. His head is tilted ever so slightly to the right. I can only imagine that inquisitive look on his face. I wonder what he could be staring at. I remember what's on the table. My heart drops, and bile rises in the back of my throat. My T-shirt begins to stick to my back. I'm pouring sweat, and a rush of adrenaline fills my veins.

"Why are there two plates of spaghetti bolognese on the table?"

He does not turn to me. I'm not sure if it's better like this or not. At least he can't see the look on my face, yet at the same time I can't see his. He knows I'm in the room.

"Ms. Bridges?" My legs are shaking.

Think, Barbara. Think!

"Fi. Fi was supposed to be coming 'round for dinner, but she had to cancel on me last minute."

Good.

"Rupert's favourite dinner is spaghetti bolognese," he says, slowly.

I know that. Of course, I know that. He's turning towards me.

Take a breath, Barbara. He knows nothing.

I pinch my cheeks, trying to bring some colour back into them. This is just a coincidence, he'll realise that, just a crazy coincidence. There's a thud from upstairs that makes the cutlery on the table rattle. Something went down, hard, and I can only imagine it's the old chest of drawers we have next to your cot.

My eyes shoot to the ceiling. I look back to Oliver, and his eyes are still on the heavens above us. He slowly brings his head down again; chin parallel with the ground. He blinks, and his eyes are on me. His eyes are darker than I thought green could go. His mossy eyes burn through every barrier I am trying to hold up. Saada is awake. Most of the street would be awake after that crash. Saada whines from the hallway. I hear her padding up the stairs, and the thud, thud of her wagging tail as it hits against the wall. There is a scratching sound as her claws come against wood, and she whines again.

"I'll go then, Ms. Bridges."

I am tense. We are tense. Our backs are stiff, and our natural postures long forgotten. I step to the side and gesture him towards the door.

Such a helpful host, am I not?

He takes one final look back at the cold plates of spaghetti before walking past me. I follow close behind him. His hand is on the latch of the door. But he's not opening it.

Why isn't he opening it?

Saada whines again from upstairs. Her scratching becomes more persistent.

Shut up, please. Don't ruin this for me all over again, Saada.

His eyes glance upstairs.

"Saada sure is worked up about something."

"I moved some things around upstairs, and I think it's upset her a bit.

"Hmm," he nods.

His eyes come back to mine, and then skirt around the hallway once more trying to pick up any sign of you. They land on the pile of shoes by the door.

"Well then, I'll go. Sorry for disturbing you. Ms. Bridges."

A scream comes from upstairs. Fists are banging against your door. Saada is howling. Oliver's eyes go as wide as an owl's in the night.

"Rupert! RUPERT!" he screams.

He pushes off the door and bolts past me. I go to grab him but only manage to catch his coat. He shrugs out of it.

"OLIVER?" You've heard him. Saada is barking madly. Oliver reaches the stairs and hits them two at a time. I lunge for him again and catch his foot. He kicks his leg free and narrowly misses my face. We're both scrambling up the stairs.

"OLIVER! SHE WON'T LET ME OUT!"

He reaches the top of the stairs and swings around to your door. I climb onto the landing just as he is opening the door. You are there, all pathetic tears and wasted water. Oliver throws himself into the room. His arms wrap around you. The door is left open. I make it to the doorway and stand there. You are hugging, so tightly you could squeeze the breath out of each other. Sobs echoing throughout the room.

I pause in the doorway catching my breath. I think I've sprained my wrist climbing up the stairs. It's throbbing. I can feel my eyelid twitching. My hair falls in clumps across my face. My breathing slows. You are still sobbing into your brother's arms. Oliver is whispering something. Words of reassurance not meant for the wicked witch to hear. I watch as the sobs slow to heavy breathing, which in turn slows to deeper, conscious breaths.

"She keeps calling me Aiden. I'm not Aiden. I'm Rupert," you say to Oliver. You peel apart and stare at me, hand in hand.

"We would like to go home now, Ms. Bridges." Oliver states.

You can't go home. I can't let you go. You'll tell others. I'll have police at the door.

"We're sorry for everything that has happened to you. But we need to go home."

You can't leave me with an empty nursery again. This is your home, now. We'll make it work. You're just a child. You'll adapt.

Oliver, squeezes your hand, knuckles white from the pressure.

Rupert? Rupert what are you doing here?

His eyes are blood red, and his face is filled with fear.

The boys make a move towards me. For a moment, I think they are coming for an embrace. I think they've forgiven me. They'll stay with me after all. But Oliver's eyes are not on mine. He's looking past me to the splices of streetlight in the hall. My body moves into his line of sight, and he pulls his brother behind him. Rupert looks out from behind with those same green eyes. The same positioning they'd once adopted on my doorstep. Yet, this time his eyes are not filled with wonder or question. They are pitted with fear.

Fear of what, My Dear? Not from me, surely not. I'm not like those monsters under your bed. I'm your protector. Stay here. I'll protect you from the big bad world. This world wasn't made for us.

Oliver stands a metre from me, and I am forced to draw my eyes from Rupert's and look to Oliver's sheer determination. My hand grips the doorframe. I can't let them leave.

We're meant for the clouds, My Dear.

"Barbara, we are going," Oliver says, with such authority and conviction in his voice.

He is less than a metre from me. I could reach out and run my hands through those thick curls. For a moment my grip on the frame softens. My jaw unclenches. Oliver's palm jolts out and with one movement he knocks my arm to the side and pushes his brother in front and past me.

"No!" I scream. "You can't leave me here again!"

I grab Oliver by the shoulder and spin him around.

"Rupert, go! Get out of the house. I'm right behind you." He turns to me. "Let us go, Barbara. We won't tell anyone about this. We *have* a family, we can't be yours as well."

Your rattle does not warm up this time around. It is loud in my ears. Saada is barking. I see your face. Your tiny, little, still face. So at peace. Eyes closed. I smell the fresh baby smell I was worried about not being able to smell from the beginning. I fall in love with you all over again as your rattle crashes around in my mind.

My grip on the boy's shoulders tightens as your image grows stronger and you begin to glow. You're glowing with this golden aura. I clench my nails in, clinging onto you for as long as I possibly can. I don't think I've ever seen you so clearly. Your long dark lashes that will melt hearts. Your smooth, rosy cheeks as perfect as the blush on a porcelain doll. You open your eyes and they are green. They are so green and so angry.

What did I do, Love? Why are you so angry?

"LET ME GO!" Oliver is in front of me; his face red with rage. I gasp.

No. Give me back my son.

"What did you do with my son?" I am shouting. My grip is getting tighter.

Your rattle is here, but your face is fading. Oliver is replacing you.

No. No. No.

I lash out. My hand connects with his face. Skin builds under my nails. I smell blood. I shake my head. Oliver screams. His hands are on his face. I look down at my own hands. Blood. All I see is blood.

"I HATE YOU!" he cries.

No.

My hands are up again. I see red, and only red. I need to get you back, Aiden. I'll do anything to get you back. My hands grow tighter. I am surprised by my own strength. It's those green eyes. Get rid of those green eyes and give me my Aiden back. Let me see his eyes. Just once, let me see them and tell them I love them.

I push my thumbs into green, consumed. A scream again. Saada barking. I push harder. Nails first. Something pops. His scream goes a pitch higher. Something hits me hard across the back of my head. Oliver's face is covered with patches of black. The power drains out of me. I release my grip. I am on my knees and can hear little baby steps running away from me.

Don't go, My Love. Don't leave me again.

"I'm sorry."

I wake up to Saada whining. She hasn't come to me. She's watching me from the top of the stairs.

Let her watch.

Thud, thud, thud. I'm drawn out of my slumber.

Thud, thud, thud. My head throbs. I reach around and feel a bump the size of a peach stone. I push myself up. Blood rushes to my head, and I have to lie back down on my side. Saada's head flicks from me to the bottom of the stairs. The door goes again. I put my hands to my face and rub my eyes.

Something isn't right. I smell copper. I look at my hands. Dried blood, flaking like paint. I pull myself to my knees, crawl into the bathroom and slowly get to my feet using the toilet seat. I lean over to the small, misted window and pull it open. Very, very slowly. I look out of the window, which sits above the front door. Rupert and Oliver are there, and their parents are at their side. Their mother is banging on the door, while the two boys hold onto their father. Oliver has a white bandage over his left eye, which is tinted red and yellow. Rupert has just started crying, and his father pulls him a little closer.

Thud, thud, thud, goes the door.

"We shouldn't be here, Audrey. Let's take the boys home. This needs to be dealt with properly."

Audrey spins around to face Jeffrey. "Oh, I'll deal with it properly, Jeffrey. I will deal with it properly." She thuds the door again on each syllable. I imagine all she sees is red. I understand. I've been there. If something like that ever happened to you, I don't think I would be as calm her. Even in her rage she is elegant. Her hair sweeps at the side of her head as she turns from our door to her family. She leans over. I hear the creak of the letterbox opening, and her voice fills our house. Saada is barking.

"Don't make us come back with the police, Barbara. The only reason I haven't so far is because the boys insisted. God knows why after what you've done to them."

I flinch as she uses my first name. "Believe me, we will go to the police if you don't let us in." The letterbox slams shut, and Saada sprints down the stairs. There is frantic whispering passing up on the wind. I can't make out what they are saying. My heart is in my throat.

How did things escalate so quickly?

I lean as close as I dare to the bathroom window.

"...if we killed her, Mum? Rupert hit her so hard. Mum? Mum, I'm worried. Mu..."

My hand goes to the bump on my head again. I don't know what to do with myself. I can feel Audrey's rage seeping up through our letterbox. *Heat rises.* I move over to the bathroom sink and turn the tap on. I lather my hands with soap and begin washing the blood off. The worst of it comes off, but my skin is stained. I'll have to soak.

"Barbara!" My name resounds through the house again.

I squeeze too tightly, and the soap pops out of my hands. Was I too loud? Can they hear the bloodied water running through the pipes? It's Oliver's voice.

"Barbara, please let us in. Mum only wants to speak to you. We want to know you're alive." I turn the tap off.

Tell me what to do, Aiden.

I suppose it's time to pick the lesser of two evils. Do I face the wrath of the law or the wrath of a mother scorned? I'm not entirely sure which is worse. I pull my hair back. I wince as I tug at the bruise on the back of my head. Running my hand over the bump, I place my hair so it falls thicker over that part of my scalp, as if that is going to help.

Thud, thud. Saada barks at the door.

"Oliver, is there a way to go around the back? Jeffrey can you go and check?"

Shit.

The patio door is unlocked. I hear the crunch on the gravel and a whimper from what I presume to be Rupert. I slowly peak my head outside the window. Jeffery has left his son behind. Rupert is hugging himself, and his brother's arm is around his shoulders. Jeffery is heading for the side gate. I look back to the bathroom mirror. My mouth is open. I sprint for the stairs as quietly as I can.

I'm dizzy. My head is spinning, and my vision blurs. I lean against the wall for a moment, but I know it's not going to take him long to figure out the latch on the side gate and make his way around. It's not going to be long until he's inside our house.

I hold onto the banister, tightly. I make my way quickly and quietly down the stairs. In my haste, I forget about the third to last step, the creak rings through the hallway like a foghorn at sea.

Thud, thud.

I don't have time to worry if Audrey's heard me or not. I have to get to that back door before Jeffrey does. I sprint through the hall and into the kitchen; my socks sliding on the floor. I almost fall over, and a second wave of dizziness hits me. I use the kitchen work surfaces for support and push off them like a swimmer from the side of a pool. With my head down, I dive for the patio door. I can imagine the boy's father turning the corner any second. I reach the door, and pushing myself against it, I slide the lock up and turn the key.

A hand is on the other side. I look up. Jeffery's arm is tense, and his hand is tight around the handle. I keep looking up, and his eyes meet mine. We are still. I got here first. His eyes flick between mine.

Fight or flight, Mr. Harp?

"Audrey!" he calls. His voice is muffled through the glazing. I hear the letterbox slam shut once again in the hallway.

"She's here! I can see her. She's here!" His eyes don't leave mine.

I'm stuck with my hand on the door handle. I'm willing my feet to move but they won't.

Come on, Barbara. Get out of here.

Audrey is at her husband's side. Her face wild, wild and beautiful. She is out of breath, and her cheeks are red. The boys join her seconds after and cower behind their protectors. They are mostly hiding behind their mother's side. I don't blame them. I'd hide behind her as well.

"She's alive!" Rupert squeals.

Audrey knocks her husband's hand aside and tries to pull the door as if this time it will open. The door pulls a little and for a second, I think she has thwarted my lock and key. But everything holds. I exhale. My eyes are on Audrey and hers are on mine. I take a step back and let go of the handle.

"Open the door, Barbara." She is determined. Her head is slightly down, and her features are narrowed.

I don't move. My heart pounds against my ribcage. She breathes out, and in that moment, I see a mother's pain in her eyes. Pain I've felt. She puts a palm to the window. My feet take me towards her and I put my palm on hers. I'm not sure if I'm imagining the heat of her body through the glass or I can actually feel it. The door is thin, and in this moment, we are simply two mothers in pain.

Before I know what my body is doing, my left hand is turning the key while my right palm stays on her left. Her right hand moves to the lock and slowly opens it from the outside. I realise what is happening and snap out of her trance. I look down and go to slide the lock back, but it's too late. The door is already opening. She slides it all the way across with such force that it vibrates as it hits the other end. I follow the door's movement with my eyes.

I don't think I've ever had it open that wide before.

I look back and there they are. Us. Our dream family. In all their beauty. Mother leading the way. Father standing as tall as he can with a hand on each child's shoulder. I look at Oliver's eye patch and turn away. Guilt floods through me.

Did I really do that?

The lump on my head starts to throb. I just wish I was on their side, that I was Audrey, and that *you* were Oliver. I wouldn't care if you had one eye or none. You would be alive. I would be avenging you against this wicked dragon that stands in the kitchen, stained with blood and wounded, inside out.

I step aside. My body going into autopilot.

"Would you like to come in?"

For a moment, each of their heads move an inch or so back like a flock of hens as they take in what I've just said. I'm pretty sure mine does the same.

What are you doing, Barbara?

Audrey is the first to move. She takes a hesitant step inside and looks around as though she were expecting some kind of sprung trap to catch her by the ankle and pull her upside down. She waves at her family to keep back, just how I imagined I would do to you as we crept down the stairs on Christmas morning.

"Santa, are you there?"

I move over to the kettle and switch it on. The boys are still standing outside like beautiful vampires waiting for their invite in. Audrey has regained her composure. She nods at her family, and they enter the kitchen but stay by the door. Ready for flight, I suppose. What more damage could I possibly do?

"Oliver, come here." she demands. Her voice slices through the air as sharp as a blade.

Jeffery let's go of his son's shoulder and gives him a gentle nudge towards his mother. His mother's arms are open towards him. Her eyes leave me for the first time, and she watches him cross all of three metres towards her like he was made of porcelain. When he reaches her, she brings him close to her, his back to her stomach, so he is facing me.

"Take off your eye patch," she whispers.

"But the doctor said I sho...'

"Just do it." She squeezes his shoulders, and I see him wince a little.

His hands move towards his face, and his other eye closes. I watch as he feels around the edges of the patch. His mouth is twisted in concentration, which as he begins to peel the patch back contorts into pain. I hold my breath.

He finishes pulling the patch back and raises his hands. The flesh surrounding his eye is inflamed, deep purple and yellow bruises cover his skin. There is fresh puss running from the inner corner, and his eye has been sewn shut like something out of a horror movie. He looks at me with the other eye, and I see the damaged one twitching beneath the lid.

"I want you to see what you've done to my son, Barbara."

"Can I put the patch back on now, Mum? The doctor said..."

"I know what the doctor said, Oliver. Put the patch back on and go and stand with your father."

Oliver does as he is told and retreats to a safe distance from this wicked beast who is capable of wicked things.

"The doctor said he might lose that eye. Can you imagine? At 13 losing an eye? Can you imagine what he'll have to go through? The pain, the trauma, operation after operation. Can you see what you've done to my child?"

The kettle pops. The water's boiled.

"Do you understand what you've done, Barbara? He'll need reconstructive surgery. Even if he can keep the eye, his vision will never be the same. Can you understand what you've done to my beautiful little baby?"

I turn back to the kettle.

"Do you take sugar, Audrey?" I busy myself in the cupboards. "I've only got white, is that okay?"

Footsteps behind me. Long strides. My hair is pulled from my scalp, and I am brought to my knees in agony. The bump on my head erupts in pain.

"Don't you feel ANYTHING?" Audrey screams in my ear. I drop the teacup.

"Audrey! Audrey, stop!" My vision blurs, but I see Jeffrey coming over to us.

"Let me show you what you've done to my boy." She still has me by the hair, and with her other hand she reaches down and picks up a piece of broken china. A pain hotter than fire slashes across my cheek. Blood is pouring from my face.

"Audrey, get off her! Calm down!"

"She doesn't feel anything, Jeffrey! I just want her to feel something. I want her to regret!" She let's go of my hair as Jeffery pulls her back.

My hand goes to my cheek. The gash is deep, and blood is pulsing through my fingers. I look up. She is crying. Her husband's hands are on her shoulders still holding her back. She's beautiful, even when she cries. She looks like an actress on camera. This woman's taking home an Oscar.

"Audrey, what have you done? How can we go to the police, now?"

Jeffrey is angry. I didn't think he could get angry. His normally soft, warm features are sharp. His brow is furrowed. He's shaking his wife's shoulders.

"I'm sorry. I'm so, so, sorry." My voice breaks in the room. I'm holding my cheek trying to stop the blood from pouring. Rupert moves towards me.

"Get away from her, Rupert." Audrey hisses.

"Let's go, Audrey." Jeffrey turns his wife towards the door. She is shaking her head. She drops the bloodied piece of china to the floor, and it clatters through the silence. They step outside. Rupert is the last to leave. He pulls the door shut. I can do nothing but watch. I am left in silence. I'm alone, surrounded by blood and a broken teacup. I look to the left and Saada is just sitting, watching me.

"What?"

She gets up and pads out of the room. I hear the creak of the third stair as she climbs her way up. I want to sit here and wallow in my pain. I'm losing blood.

I head up the stairs. I pass your room and Saada is curled in a ball by your cot with her head on her paws and her eyes closed. I pull your door closed. I reach the bathroom mirror. Pinkish water is still in the sink. There's been far too much blood spilled today. I look in the mirror. The wound stretches from just below my right eye down to my jaw. The flesh has been spliced clean through. I need to go to the hospital. This will need stitches. This will scar. I want this to scar. I want to remember this and the pain I have caused. I need to.

⏤⏤⏤⏤⏤⏤⏤⏤⏤⏤⏤⏤⏤

The blood has stopped pulsing out of the gash on my cheek, and I'm sitting in the corridor of A&E holding a towel to my face. People are whizzing past me. Doctors are buzzing around in their lab coats, saving time, and saving lives. People have come and gone. Children sit with their mothers, some are crying, and others are sitting in a stony silence. Couples. So many couples rowing, hugging, laughing, and on phones talking to others.

One dainty little woman comes in with a baby. It's so tiny in her arms; it can't be more than six months old. She doesn't last in the corridor long. I'm not sure how long I've been here. It just seems like people are coming and going and everyone's overlooking us. Maybe they know what I did? Maybe this is my punishment. My jaw aches, but I don't want to move it because I'm scared blood will start pouring through once again.

A little girl dressed as a Disney princess sits opposite me with a bloodied nose. Her lovely blue dress is stained with blood, and she's holding a pink napkin to her nose. Her legs are swinging from her seat, and she's twirling a wand with a star on the end of it in her free hand. Her parents are talking over her head:

"I told you to watch her. You can't leave them alone for a second." the mother said.

"I did watch her!"

"Really, Dave? Were you watching her or that bloody phone again? What do you even do on it that's so important?"

"Clare, chill. I was..."

"I've told you time and time again that the two of them together are no good. Her brother's a bad influence on her."

"What did you say about me, Mum? Catch!" A boy in his late teens strolls around the corner. His left arm is in a cast, covered in multi-coloured scribbles. He throws a can of soda at his dad.

"Jesus Christ, Rick!" Dave, the dad, barely catches the can. Clutching it to his chest like a rugby ball.

"Dave! Seriously? There are children everywhere, keep your cursing to a minimum. I'm sure these people think we're bad enough parents as it is."

"Mum?" The teen goes to throw another can to her. The mother yelps and flaps her arms in front of her. The boy never actually intended to throw it. I think he just wanted to scare her. But the can slips out of his hand. His instinct is to reach out and try to grab it with both hands. He winces in pain as he tries to move his broken arm and just slaps the can to the floor. It bursts open and fizz sprays the can in circles.

"For fuck's sake, Rick!" His dad is up on his feet trying to grab the can.

"Dave! What did I just say?" the mother scolded. The teen quickly sits in his father's seat and slips out a lollipop from the pocket of his hoodie.

"The doctor said I've been a good boy." He winks at his sister as he passes her over the lollipop.

She grins up at him with sheer adoration. The tissue and wand fall to her lap as she unwraps the lolly and quickly puts it into her mouth. Her legs swing a little bit faster. Her nose is puffy and purple, yet she turns to look at me with pure content. Her father is scrambling around on the floor. Her mother is bickering away with her brother over her head. All the while she sits there, at peace with her lollipop. She smiles, a gap-toothed smile at me. A flower in a hurricane.

"Ms. Bridges?"

I break my gaze with the girl as a young female doctor calls me. *They're just getting younger and younger.*

I wince at the sentence that I heard my own mother say so many times when I was a child.

They are not getting younger, Mother. We're just getting older and refusing to admit it.

"Are you okay to walk or do you want me to grab a chair?" Was she patronising me? I took myself here on the No. 39. I think I can handle a short stroll down a corridor. I stand. She turns on her heels and leads the way. *Clip, Clop* like a horse and cart on a wedding day.

Clip Clop. There goes the bride. Shower her in rice.

I'm not sure if you're still allowed to throw rice at weddings? I heard the birds eat it, and then it swells in their stomachs making them explode from inside out. I follow the doctor into her office and that's all it is. Nothing as fancy as my last doctor's. I guess that's a good thing though, right? They haven't clocked onto who I am yet.

Clip Clop. Shower me with rice.

"Take a seat please, Ms. Bridges. Sorry to keep you waiting, but we must prioritise the need of our patients. You seem like quite a tough cookie. How are you feeling?" A tough cookie I may be, but 12 years old I am not. I take the seat and smile at her.

"Right, let's take a look at you, shall we?"

Let's.

She snaps on some blue gloves and slowly pulls my hands away from the towel. She is now holding the towel to my face and stands up looking down on me as she slowly peels the towel away from my cheek. I am stuck with her breasts in my face and don't really know where else I can look. Her lab coat is open and has blocked my vision on either side, like a horse with blinders. So, I stare at her breasts. They are the colour of the darkest cocoa. I wait for her to assess the damage.

"Ouch. How did you manage to do this one, Ms. Bridges?" I hadn't thought about that question. Luckily for me it was rhetorical, for now.

"We're going to need some stitches in that and to give it a good clean up. I must say, it will probably scar, but if we get this cleaned up pronto, there shouldn't be any infection. How long ago did it happen?"

"Earlier tonight," I whisper as she pulls away from me and takes a seat back at her desk. I don't think she's wearing a bra.

She removes her gloves and begins typing away at a computer. Its screen is taking up most of her desk and is facing away from me.

Tap, tap, tap. The rice hits the floor.

"And…how did it happen? What caused the laceration?"

I'm quiet for a little while, but there's no way to avoid this. The tapping stops. She is looking at me.

She's definitely not wearing a bra.

"It was a piece of china from a broken teacup." I look at the hospital bed in the room. I'm suddenly obsessed with anything other than the doctor's eyes and breasts.

"Okay..." She strings out the end of the word as she types away. You can tell she's curious. Can you blame her? I've cut my face open with a broken teacup. Surely, that's a first?

Tap, tap.

"Ms. Bridges, I have to ask." Her eyes are trained on me, her ripe lips tight as she leans forward in her chair. Her top falls down a little.

"How did it happen?"

I briefly look up from her breasts to her eyes and then back down.

Where do I begin?

"I do need you to tell me how it happened, Ms. Bridges. I can assure you it will be kept in confidence between you and I, unless I think you're at a greater risk. But I won't do anything without your knowledge first."

My hands are fidgeting, climbing over each other in my lap. Maybe this cookie is beginning to crumble after all.

"I got into a fight."

I reach her eyes once more, and I see her glance down to my hands. I think she's assessing my nerves. I try to hold still. She looks back up, and her attitude towards me has changed. She is a little more abrasive. She leans back in her chair and crosses her hands on her lap.

"May I ask with whom?" She was looking for a ring. She is categorizing me. Desperate girlfriend gets in row with her boyfriend until he beats her.

"It was with a friend. We fell out over something...something stupid, and things got out of hand. You don't have anything to worry about. Honestly, I'm not at risk."

"Well, I have to tell you, I don't know many friends that attack each other with china. My days never fail to surprise me in this place." Her last sentence was said more to herself rather than me as she shook her head.

"Right then, would you mind going to lay down on that bed, and we'll get you patched up." She turns back to her computer and begins tapping away once more. What more could she possibly have to say?

"I'm going to prescribe you some painkillers and something to help with the swelling. We'll have to do quite a few stitches. Luckily, I've got a steady hand, so they shouldn't hurt too much. They're dissolvable ones, as well, so when they're ready, they'll disintegrate, and your body will naturally push them out."

She snaps back on her gloves, after she's finished typing and comes over to me on the hospital bed. She switches this huge sun of a light on and points it directly at my face. I see spots.

"Perhaps it's time you found some new friends, Ms. Bridges."

I walk out of her room, my face pulled tight with stitches. I'm pretty sure I look like I've been attacked, which I guess is accurate for what actually happened. Still, you don't see women my age walking around with a face full of stitches. In general, we're a little more careful. I notice the little girl in her princess dress and her mother have been summoned leaving the boys to be boys. The father is punching the son at the top of his broken arm, asking if he feels anything. The son is in hysterics. I really don't see what's so funny about it, but if he's making his son happy, then good luck to him. There's a sticky brown stain on the floor and not a soda can in sight.

I'm not sure what will happen next with Oliver and Rupert. I don't know if I'll have police waiting for me on my doorstep when I return home. Maybe I'll never hear from any of them again. I remember Rupert moving towards me after his mother had attacked me. Perhaps it was a final act of kindness, it's a gesture I'd like to hold onto. A parting gift. After everything I have put him through. I held him hostage in your room and he still felt sorry for me. I'm crying as I exit the hospital. Most people look at me, see the scar on my face and realise I am not worth the hassle. I am not someone worthy of their attention. My phone goes, and Fi's name flashes up on the screen.

"Hey, Fi."

"Hey, Barbara. How's things?"

Good question.

"Things are okay. I'm just leaving the hospital now." I continue before she has a chance to start judging. "Don't worry, I'm fine. No more drugs, and no more breakdowns. Well, a few more drugs, but they're only painkillers. I fell in the kitchen and sliced my face open." I back it up with an "I'm such a klutz" chuckle.

Buy it, Fi.

"How do you mean you fell over? You fell over what? Wait. You sliced your face open? Did you fall into the dishwasher or something?" She was being sarcastic, but that is gold. I don't know why I didn't think of that.

"Exactly."

"Barbara. You don't have a bloody dishwasher!"

Fair point.

"You haven't been 'round for a while, Sis. I bought one a week or so ago. It's really fancy. Did you know you can wash your dishes in seven different ways?"

Buy it, Fi. Please.

"Well, look at you, Ms. Bigshot. I hope you're saving some money for my Christmas present?" I force another chuckle. "Anyway, look. I'm thinking of bringing the boys over at the weekend. They are so desperate to see you and Saada after everything I've told them. Plus, I have something I really need your advice on, but I can't talk now. Can you squeeze us in at some point?"

"Sure, it'll be good to see the boys, too. It's been way too long. Come over for dinner on Saturday, if you'd like."

"Perfect. Jack has turned veggie on me, just a heads up. He's just seen *Chicken Run*. It should probably be over by the weekend though."

"Meat all around then. I'll see you then, Fi."

"See you then. Oh, and Barbara?"

"Tell me."

"I love you." I smile a genuine smile.

"I love you, too. See you Saturday." I close the conversation and open a web tab on my phone. Looks like Mummy needs to buy a dishwasher.

I missed my stop on the bus journey home. I spent the entire trip reading bad reviews on poorly designed dishwashers. I spent a ridiculous amount of time looking for angry mums concerned for the safety of their children. I needed to find a dishwasher capable of doing these horrific things to my face. A villain of a dishwasher. Plus, this particular villain needs to be affordable. I haven't checked on my funds for a long time. I just hope that every time I use my card it will work. I walked back on myself a good 10 minutes extra at the end of my journey. I found my perfect partner in crime, and she comes with next day delivery and free installation. Perfect.

I let myself in quietly. Afraid of breaking the peace in my own home. I feel like I'm entering a library or a morgue. Take your pick. The hallway smells funny. Something is off. Perhaps, something's gone rotten in the bin. I head into the kitchen and allow the night's events to replay in my head. There is a huge sense of finality among the events.

Something tells me I won't be seeing the Harps again. This thought is both comforting and unnerving. I know it's for the better. If I do manage to avoid having the police involved in my business, then I'll have a very lucky escape. Justice will have to wait for another day. I grab a broom from the drying cupboard and begin sweeping up the broken teacup. The white sugar is still sitting on the work surface. Audrey's words replay through my head as I sweep.

"He'll need reconstructive surgery."

I think I've got it all until I stand on another shard with my heel.

"Don't you feel ANYTHING?"

I do, Audrey. I really do. I feel it all now. I let her words echo around the room as my eyes fall on the last bloodied piece of china nearer the door. I feel everything, and it feels amazing. I let the tears roll as I pick up the piece of china. This is exactly what I need.

I drop the last piece of china into the bin and pause for a moment. I breathe in deep, deep breaths. I need to remember this feeling. I need to remember that this *is* a feeling. I am half expecting your rattle to sound, but I hear nothing.

Wait? That's a lie. I heard something. *Saada.* Saada, bless her. I'd closed her in your room. How many hours ago was that now? 12? 13? I turn on my heels and head for the stairs.

"Saada? Honey, are you ok?" I call out, expecting a bark. The whining is growing louder, but that's only because I'm getting closer. The putrid smell hits the back of my throat and makes me gag as I reach the top of the stairs.

Oh Saada, I'm so sorry.

I slowly open your door, not entirely sure what to expect. Saada is sitting in the corner of the room trying to be as small as she possibly can be. Her mess is all over the carpet. She whimpers and stands with her tail between her legs, and her head hanging low. She walks past me and plods down the stairs. I cannot deal with this now. Guilt riddles through me. I close your door and follow her downstairs. She's pawing at the patio door. I let her outside, and she vomits in the back garden. I go to refill her dog bowl before taking my tired self upstairs to bed.

Happy Birthday, son. I miss you.

Dear Aiden,

The deliveryman turned his nose up as soon as he entered the front door. I made a mental note to clean up your room before Fi arrives at the weekend. But, we have a dishwasher! The lengths I would go to in hopes that I could convince your aunty that I'm okay are ridiculous. With the dishwasher installed, I felt a few hundred pounds lighter, and I was looking forward to the weekend.

I also decided to email Dan to ask for my job back. I was with them for five years prior to you. I hoped Dan would remember that when he read my email. I needed to show him I'm competent enough to come back to work...that I am able.

Dear Dan,
As you know, the last two years haven't been kind to me.

Hi Dan,
How are you? I was just wondering...Sorry to bother you...

Dan,
Thanks for your patience.

I didn't even know how to begin writing something like this.
I finally settled with:

> "Dan,
> *Do you mind if I stop by at some point next week?*
> *Thanks,*
> *Barbara*"

I don't exactly want to go back to work. I'm not entirely sure
we're ready. We have so many memories there and I'm not sure
if I can handle reliving them. However, I need to try. We have
dishwashers to pay for and lives to live. I think back to the times
in the office when you were just *Bump*. Am I ready to trigger
those memories again? Will I ever be ready? To my surprise, Dan
replied straight away. It was probably the quickest response I've
ever had from him:

> "Hi Barbara,
> *Pleased to hear from you. I hope you are doing well?*
> *How does Wednesday sound? I'm free first thing.*
> *Sending my love from all of us at the office.*
> *Dan*"

Booked.

I needed to deal with your room next. I needed everything
to be in place for Aunty Fi. No more nasty surprises. I headed
up the stairs, and the smell seemed so much worse. I opened
the door, and it almost knocked me back. How could one dog
create so much mess? I grabbed some cleaning products from
the bathroom and got to work. I kept gagging at the smell, but

everything needed to come out. I always knew carpet was a bad idea for a baby's nursery, but I just couldn't resist at the time. I hardly expected to be cleaning dog mess from it. Baby food, yes. Spilt milk, yes. Baby vomit, yes. But, never this.

I managed to reduce Saada's mess to faint yellow stains. The room smelt of cleaning products. I went to the chest of drawers that Rupert pulled to the floor and pushed it back against the wall. I picked up a few loose items that had fallen out of the top drawers. Nappies, a blue towel and a bottle of talcum powder. I placed them back in the drawer. I was all too aware of how easy it would be to let these items consume me again. Instead, I distanced myself from my thoughts. I needed to stay on track for our visitors at the weekend. I held on to the talcum powder before twisting the lid and returning to the yellow stains. I squeezed the bottle hard, and plumes of talcum powder rained down onto the carpet. It smelt better immediately. It smelt new again. I gave the room a few more puffs of talc before tucking the bottle back into the top drawer.

That'll do.

I went downstairs to the front room. There was one more thing I needed to deal with before Fi's boys arrived. Your presents were still sitting haphazardly against the wall. It was time I moved them. I'm sorry, Love. It's not that I love you any less. I just know what Fi's boys are like. Your presents won't last two minutes once they're here. I don't want to spend the afternoon fending off prying hands.

I took the presents up to your room one by one, as if each one was filled with glass. I kept my chin up and hummed the same song that was in my head when I emptied our locker all those months ago. It comforted me. I straightened up some bows and tucked loose wrapping back in its place. We'll open these one day, Love. I promise.

Your nursery seemed a lot smaller and our living room a lot bigger. Who knew we had so much space down here? There was a collection of right-angled dust lines in the carpet, like someone played an awful game of Tetris across the floor. I decided to take care of that later. I need to sleep now. Good night, My Love.

5th August

Dear Aiden,

I woke up to a blood-stained pillow and thought I was in a nightmare. My wound opened up in the night. I must have scratched it because my face was throbbing. I headed straight into the bathroom and tried to clean as much of my face as I could without pulling at the stitches. Once I managed to get my face in order, I went back to my room and changed the sheets. I wanted everything to be spotless for Fi's arrival. I remember the days when I thought nothing of her visits, the days when she wouldn't even tell me she was coming over. She had her own key and just let herself in. In fact, she still has her own key; she just chose to stop letting herself in.

The doorbell rang at two o'clock, sharp. She was actually on time for once. I knew something must have been wrong.

Smile.

I opened the door.

Fi was turned, facing her two boys:

"Remember what I said," she whispered to them before turning to me. Her face dropped as soon as she saw me, and I remembered how I must have looked.

"Barbara! Your beautiful face!" The boys raced around their mother and threw their arms around my waist.

"We missed you, Aunty Barbara."

"I don't care what your face looks like, Aunty Barbara."

"I actually think it looks cool. Is it gonna scar, Aunty Barbara?"

"Fred! What did Mum say?" Fred looked up at me sheepishly after being scolded by his older brother. Although Jack was actually only two and a half minutes older, he always seemed like he was years ahead. I pried the boys' hands away from my hips and knelt down to their level.

"I'm pleased you don't care what my face looks like, Jack. Fred, the doctor told me that it will probably scar, but it shouldn't be too bad." I smiled at them. "And, I've missed you both as well."

I put one hand on each of their shoulders and held them at arm's length. They wore matching striped tops and cargo shorts. Their socks were too big for their legs and fell in clusters at their ankles. The boys had most of their mother's features—dark brown hair and eyes to match. Their skin was lightly freckled, and they had dimples that I could spend the winter in. They also inherited the one thing we feared they'd get from their father—a hooked nose.

"Now, I know I'm going to sound just like Nana when I say this, but my, haven't you grown!" I put on my best elderly accent, and the boys giggled back at me and rolled their eyes. "How old are you now, 15? 16?" They laughed again.

"You know we're only eight, Aunty Barb! Mum says we're going on 15 though."

"Come on then, let's get you inside. I've got someone I'd like you both to meet." The boys squealed their excitement.

I took the three of them through to the kitchen and stood alongside the dishwasher. Fi gave a nod of acknowledgement towards my new appliance.

Fantastic, that topic is out of the way.

She lugged a bag over to the kitchen table.

"I'll be right back, I've got another two in the car. I couldn't trust the boys with it." She disappeared, and the boys stood at attention by the patio door.

"Why are you two so quiet then, eh?" I turned towards them.

"Mummy said we're not to give you a hard time." Jack's voice went up a note as he mimicked his mother.

"Well, that does sound very much like your mother. But that doesn't mean you can't be yourselves. I could do with some noise around here."

The boys looked at each other, communicating how only twins can. Your cousins can say a thousand words with one look at each other. It's a gift.

"Mum said you haven't been very happy lately, and the last thing you need is us two giving you grief."

"Oh, don't you worry, Lovelies, I've had enough grief for a lifetime. I don't think anything you two do could be worse than what I've been through."

Too much?

"We miss Aiden, too, even though we never got to meet him. We were super excited though. We'd planned all the places we wanted to take him. We put together all our old toys and clothes for him, too."

"I was going to give him my Scalextric." Fred said.

"Thanks for your help boys, I've got this," Fi said sarcastically as she walked back into the room with two bags packed full of food and drink, shattering the intimate moment. She looked over at us.

"Did I interrupt something? Boys, I hope I didn't interrupt anything." Her tone was stern. I turned to my sister, shaking my head.

"Not at all, Little Miss Nosey. I was just warning the boys about Saada and our no-go words."

"No-go words?" Fred looked up at me, bewildered.

Smooth, Fred.

"Really? What are they?" Fi challenged the boys, while placing the bags on the kitchen table and putting one hand on her hip.

"Walk, Poop and Chorizo. You should know that by now, Fi." I replied for the boys before they even had a chance to show their ignorance. "Right, now that's out of the way, are you two ready to meet her?" I turned back to them. They were both nodding at me with smiles as wide as their faces.

"Let's go, then." I slid the patio door open. Before the boys even had a chance to step outside, Saada came bounding into the house with her tongue lolling out the side of her mouth. She jumped on the two boys, who loved every second.

"That's them out of the way for the night. Come and help me unpack will you, Sis? I brought you goodies!"

We unpacked bread, meats, cheeses, vegetables, rice, wine, wine, and more wine. Anyone watching would have thought they were moving in.

"Fi, how long are you planning on staying?" I laughed. "I hope you don't intend to get through all this wine tonight?"

"I just thought I'd stock you up a little. You and I both know there's no such thing as too much wine." She winked at me over the mountain of food as I began filling the cupboards.

Here comes another one, just doing their part.

I took my hand and literally brushed away the bitterness I'd just mounted against my sister. I should have been thankful I had anyone left after what I've done.

"Put the oven on, will you?" she asked.

We pottered about the kitchen, prepping food, and sipping wine. Fi put the radio on, and we danced with the boys when they eventually came back in from the garden. It was harmless, and it was exactly what I needed—normality. The boys soon retreated to the front room with Saada. I tensed as they opened the door, expecting questions to come flying out.

Who are all these presents for?

Can we open one, Aunty Barb? Please?

I held my breath, but no questions came, and the boys soon dozed off with Saada laying across their laps. It took a moment for me to remember where your presents were. I walked back into the kitchen after checking up on them. Fi had put plates in the oven to warm while our casserole sat cooling on the side.

"He's cheating on me, Barbara."

"What?"

"Joey...he's cheating on me."

This wasn't what I was expecting when she told me she had news. My sister stood in front of me, holding up her hands covered in oven mitts and her eyebrows scooping to the centre of her forehead. I had a flashback to when she thought she had PVA'd her hands. It was years ago, when we were children. Our parents went crazy because Fi got her hands on some industrial superglue instead of PVA. The same look of pure sadness as she realised the pain she'd have to go through to get the glue off her hands was now plastered across her face.

"I was showering in the en suite, and I closed the door because the boys were reading with him in our bed. The mirror fogged up. See you soon, it said. With an X underneath." Her hands were still in the air. Her elbows were tucked into her sides. "See you soon." She looked at me, seven years old all over again.

"Oh, Fi."

"See you soon," she repeated.

She let out a sob and covered her mouth with an oven mitt as tears streamed down her face. I rushed across the kitchen, took her onto my shoulder and stroked her hair. I used to do the same thing to help her fall asleep when our worlds were dark and filled with monsters.

Maybe they still were.

She eventually pulled away from me.

"She's been in our house, Barb. She's been in our bed. I've slept on the same sheets as her. God knows how many times."

"Oh, Love." I shook my head, staring into her eyes, wishing it all better. I headed to the fridge.

"What am I going to do about the boys, Barb? Our little boys."

I opened a fresh pack of jelly cubes and offered her one. She took it from me and popped it in her mouth and washed it down like a painkiller with a large swig of wine.

"We'll figure something out. Have you said anything to him?" I put a jelly cube in my own mouth. She shook her head.

"I cleaned the bathroom mirror."

I nodded my approval. She took another cube from the pack.

"Can we stay with you tonight?" Now, that I didn't expect. I was nodding before I knew what I was agreeing to.

"I have a change of clothes for all of us in the car. The boys don't know yet. Joey doesn't either. It'll be just like when we were kids." She nodded at me through the tears, encouraging me to say yes.

"Fi? Fi, Love. Stop. Of course, you can stay as long as you need. I can put the boys on the sofa, and we can share like old times. You don't need to convince me."

"I love you," she said.

"I love you, too. Now, let's eat before this masterpiece goes cold."

She laughed, and a snot bubble formed and burst onto my face. She laughed again, wiping her eyes and dabbing away mascara streaks.

"I'll go get the boys," I said. I waited in the hallway to give her a moment before I woke up Jack and Fred. I heard her sigh, followed by the clatter of cutlery as she fished the plates out of the oven.

"Boys, wakey, wakey." They rubbed their tired eyes and shook awake at the same time as Saada. "Time for dinner."

Bleary eyed and still half asleep, they climbed off the sofa and marched into the kitchen like zombies.

"Well, don't all rush at once you two. It's not like me and Aunty Barbara have been cooking this for you all afternoon."

They sat at the table.

"What is it?" Fred yawned as Jack slapped his own cheeks and shook his face to wake himself up.

"Pork and pear casserole," Fi replied.

"Eew!" Fred grimaced.

"Fred Robert Leonardo, that is no way to talk about your aunt's cooking."

"Boys, remember I made this half and half with your mummy. So if you really don't like it, don't blame just me."

"I'm serious, Barb, I won't have them being so rude."

"Daddy makes faces at your cooking all the time," Fred said.

"Daddy doesn't realise how lucky he is. Daddy will realise how fantastic Mummy's cooking is when it's too late and Mummy won't cook for Daddy anymore."

The boys were still a few steps behind, pulling dreams from their reality and choosing what memories they wanted to hold on to.

"What?" Fred replied.

"Nothing," Fi shook her head. "Take your finger out of your nose, go wash your hands and then eat.'

"Sorry Mummy, I didn't mean to make you upset." I looked across at Fi who had fresh tears running down her face.

"Mummy's not upset. It's just the onions, they're really strong."

"Mummy's been eating a lot of onions lately," Jack said, as he began picking at his dinner. We both looked at him.

"They don't miss a thing, do they?" Fi said, laughing a little through the tears.

"We can hear you," Fred called from the sink.

"No, you can't. You can't hear us if we're not talking to you," Fi replied.

"Watch, Barbara. I bet they can't eat all of their dinner. You know that if they don't, then they can't have any of our ice cream."

The boys took the bait. Fred ran back to the table and the pair began shoving their dinner down their throats. The same tactic was used on us as kids, except we would slip our vegetables out the window when our parents had their backs turned.

"Boys, how would you feel if I told you that we're going to spend a little more time with Saada and Aunty Barbara this weekend?"

"That would be cool! We love Saada, don't we Jack?" Fred elbowed his brother in the ribs.

"We love Aunty Barbara, too," Jack added. Fred nodded his approval and shovelled another forkful of food into his mouth.

Fi caught my eye. "Watch this," she mouthed.

"How do you boys feel about a sleepover?"

Jack almost spat his food back on his plate. Fred threw his hands into the air, and a forkful full of mashed potato flew up next to the spotlight on the ceiling. We all looked up and watched as the mashed potato peeled away from the ceiling and hit the floor with an audible slop. Saada whipped in and devoured it before we had a chance to react. We burst out laughing.

"I need to get me one of those!" Fi said through teary eyes. The boys joined the laughter, presuming they weren't in trouble for flinging mashed potato across the kitchen.

"Are you serious though, Mum?" Jack asked. "Are we actually going to have a sleepover? Can we stay up until ten?"

"Yes, I'm serious and only if your plates are so clean by the time you're done that I can put them directly back into the cupboards."

The boys refocused their attention on their meals, and Fi raised her glass to me. We giggled and took a swig of wine.

After dinner we picked a film and sat on the floor of the living room sharing a tub of ice cream between us. The boys fell asleep 15 minutes in with a sticky layer of dried ice cream around their mouths. Fi and I worked together to slip off their clothes and tuck them in on the sofa for the night. Saada lay between them on the floor guarding their sugar-riddled dreams. As the boys' toes twitched, we pulled the door closed and headed up to bed.

We didn't say a word as we prepared for bed with bellies full of food, love and wine. We shared the bathroom sink as we brushed our teeth, just like when we were younger. We eventually dragged our weary souls into bed and lay across from each other. The streetlight cast a yellow glow over my sister's face. She was too good for this world. I could see that clearly.

"Barb?"

"Mm?" I replied, my eyes heavy.

"I'm leaving him, Barb."

"Yeah?"

"How can I ever trust him again?" she whispered. "He's not the man I knew."

"They never are, Love."

"I just..."

I think I must have dozed off for a second because I don't remember what she said next. She stroked my arm and I came back around. "I hope he'll think of me as much as I'll think of him. I hope he hurts, too. I hope he'll regret destroying our family."

"I'm sure he will, Fi." I stifled a yawn. "He'll think about you more than you know. Don't let anyone tell you otherwise."

"I love you," she whispered, and everything went dark.

6th August

Dear Aiden,

The twins came bounding into our bedroom this morning. It felt good to be surrounded by family again. You cannot fault their happiness or their enthusiasm. We were dragged out of bed and ordered to get ready for the day. The sun shone bright through the bathroom window, and the water from the shower washed last night's wine away. Fi gave the boys their overnight bags this morning and ordered them to brush their teeth twice as long because they missed it last night.

We decided to go out for breakfast and found ourselves in a small bakery we used to visit with your nana. The boys sat with their hands wrapped around a glass of orange juice. Fi and I cuddled a cappuccino each. We all had a jam and cheese croissant for old times' sake.

"I'm going back to the office next week," I said, while dabbing my finger on croissant crumbs and moving them from the table back to my plate.

"Have you spoke to Dan already?"

"Yeah, he told me to stop by on Wednesday."

Fi was silent for a moment as she digested the information with the last of her croissant.

"Well, this is great. This is what you need, to get back to normality."

I nodded, finding it hard to swallow.

"Honestly, I don't want to do it, Fi. But I have to. I'm just scared."

"What are you scared of?"

"Memories."

We both fell silent again. I had no doubt she was reliving the days after I lost you. The days when she had to pick me up after worried calls from disturbed co-workers. I was thinking more of the memories before you were taken from me. Those memories were always so easy to relive and get lost in.

"Memories can be a good thing, Barbara. They make us who we are. We have to remember what we've been through to be where we are today. We have to learn from them."

"Okay, what did they put in your coffee because I need some of that."

"Mummy took three sugars this morning and she's only supposed to have one," Fred piped up, not taking his eyes away from his croissant.

Fi threw a warning glance to her son.

"Thank you for sharing, Fred." She turned back to me. "I'm serious though, Barb. Face the memories. Don't ignore them. Live through them. The good, the bad and the gross. You can't run from your past."

I wasn't sure if she was talking about me or herself. She continued to stir her coffee.

"You're right. Well, it's only a meeting. Nothing formal. I just want to see how I feel being back in that environment. If it feels good, then I'll ask if he has anything for me."

"We'll stay with you until Wednesday," Fi stated.

We both knew it was going to be tough for me, but it was something I had to do. She was completely right, Aiden. I need to start putting the past behind me. This doesn't mean I need to forget. Trust me, I never want to forget you. But I do need to start moving on. After everything that happened with the Harp boys, it's about time I start taking control of our lives once again. I need to make sure that when I see you next, I'll make you proud. I want to have stories that will make you realise where you got your heart of gold.

9th August

Aiden,

The last few days with Fi and the boys whipped past me. Today crept up on me every time my back was turned, like a game of *What's the Time, Mr. Wolf?*

When Fi and I were in secondary school we took turns helping each other get ready in the morning. Over dinner the night before, we would weigh up who had a more important day, and that person would get privileges the following morning. There would never be a fight or an argument, just a discussion. Our mother couldn't believe how civilly we organised our mornings. Your nana was one of 13 girls, Aiden. Can you imagine that? Thirteen girls and only one brother, the poor thing. I imagine she grew up in a very different household than the one she created.

If we decided I needed the most help getting ready, then Fi would sneak into my room and wake me up five minutes before my alarm was due to go off. She'd slip into bed with me and turn off my alarm. Then she would stroke my hair, luring me away from my dreams. We'd lay in bed for a little longer and dissect the bleary images we could recall from the night before. Maybe I had a quiz or a presentation. Or, maybe it was something as important as having a lunch date with classmates I wanted to start hanging out with. Eventually, I would head to the shower and Fi would lay out accessories she considered appropriate for the occasion.

Today was no different from those days, except then, the worst of our worries was having prickly legs or skirts that were too short. I was awoken by Fi's fingers running through my hair. She had pulled open the blinds a little, and the morning light set the backs of my eyelids aglow. For a moment, in between sleep and reality, you were not there. Fi's boys were not there. Oliver and his family were not there. It was just me and Fi. We were kids again, naïve to the world and all the surprises it had in store for us. I woke up smiling.

"How are you feeling, Barb?" Her voice rang through my head, deeper than I remembered, and I left the last dreams of our past behind.

"I'm okay," I said, slapping my lips together and rubbing the sleep out of my eyes.

"Ready for your big day?"

A stone dropped in my stomach.

Was it really Wednesday, already?

"No," I replied, honestly.

"Jump in the shower. I'm going to go and plate up breakfast."

I nodded and climbed out of bed and Fi went downstairs. I bathed. We ate without talking, and the clanging of cutlery chimed through the kitchen. Two very tired looking boys eventually joined us at the table. I sat watching them spill ketchup down their fronts while Fi headed upstairs.

"Barbara?" she called. "I don't want to panic you, but you have 30 minutes before you need to leave."

"Mummy shouldn't be shouting from upstairs," Jack said.

"You're in one room, we're in another," Fred mocked. I couldn't help but smile at their innocence. I'd give anything to have that back. I'd give everything to see you have it.

There were three outfits laid across my bed, including clothes I didn't even realise I had. Everything looked so formal. Was this really what I used to wear? None of this said anything about me. But then, what would say something about me now? My stretched *Roger Rabbit* pyjama top? My black winter coat still stained with blood from my fall? What about Audrey's bottle of perfume on my windowsill? I picked out the lesser of the demons, and Fi nodded her approval as she began to pack away the rest of the clothes.

"I don't want you to agree to anything you don't want to today, Barb."

"Mhmm."

"But, I also don't want you getting your hopes up. He may just be showing an act of good faith. He may not even want to talk to you about work but just want to check up on you."

There it was again, another noble Samaritan doing their part to make the world a better place.

"Mhmm."

"Whatever happens today, the boys and I will be ready for you after, okay? Do you want me to give you a lift in? Barb?"

I finally put the last of my outfit together—a grey skirt suit and a light blue blouse. I looked at myself in the mirror, smoothing my skirt over my thighs. Was it too much? It was definitely tighter than I remembered.

"Barbara? Stay with me." Fi came up behind me and brushed the shoulders of the jacket down like a fine tailor admiring her own work. "You forgot that you can scrub up pretty well, huh?"

I didn't reply. Instead I let Fi twist and pull my hair until she tamed it back.

"Stay there, I'm going to grab my makeup bag." Before I could object, Fi was out of the room, and I did exactly as I was told. I stayed there, still, until she returned.

"Nothing too much, Fi, please."

"I'm just going to put a little mascara here..." She trailed off, her tongue poked out in concentration.

My field of vision was filled with her face. I watched her eyes at work as her brows knotted into a frown. She stepped back and gave me a once over, with her mascara brush poised, ready for round two. Without taking her eyes off me, she pulled another brush from her bag and furiously ran it along my cheeks.

"Fi, I'm serious. I don't want to look like I've tried too hard. It'll be embarrassing."

"That's it, I'm done." She took a step to the side, hands raised in submission, and I looked at her handy work in the mirror.

"Oh."

"Is that a good oh or a bad oh?"

"I don't look like me."

"Incorrect. You look exactly like the you that you used to be. It's a good thing, Barbara."

"Mmm." My face looked alive. There was definition to my cheekbones, and my eyes were framed with beautiful long lashes that I'd forgotten about.

"Now, do you want a lift in or are you getting the bus? Because if you wanted to get the bus you probably should have left five minutes ago."

"It's okay, I'll get the bus."

"But you'll be late."

"You forget how many years I worked there, Fi. I was never late, and I've left the house a lot later than this before."

"That's my girl." She smiled at me before pushing me out of my bedroom. "Go get 'em, Sis. I'm so proud of you. You have no idea."

The boys ran out from the kitchen as I slipped my shoes on by the front door.

"Bye, Aunty Barbara," they sung in unison, their voices perfectly complementing each other's. I closed the door feeling like I could take on anything the world threw at me. I had a newfound confidence I thought I'd lost in the hospital all that time ago. Yet there I was, Son, making you proud. It was all for you. It will always be for you.

I reached the office with seven minutes to spare. I stood outside the building, which looked a lot bigger than I remembered. Memories of my first interview came rushing back. Perhaps I was wearing the same suit I'm wearing now? My mind jumped back to the days before you were with us, before you were even visible. I had dreamt about you since I was young. I daydreamed for hours about how perfect we would be together, strolling down the street with you laughing on my hip. I used to fantasize over the names I would call you. If you were a girl, I would have named you Jessica or Elizabeth or something royal-sounding. For years, I wanted to call you Jason, until I was 22 and started dating a Jason. Mummy doesn't like Jasons anymore.

I took a few deep breaths just like I practised on the bus and entered the office. The front desk girls greeted me. Their beauty reminded me of the Sirens from Greek mythology—three beautiful sea-nymphs that sat on a rock in the middle of the sea and sang to sailors who may have lost their way. The story says that the sailors would hear their song and fall in love. They'd veer their boats off course and head towards the rock, where they would eventually catch sight of the wicked birdlike women before crashing to their watery graves.

"Barbara!" they cooed in unison. All three of them, luring me towards the rocks.

Put cotton in my ears.

They flurried around me, ruffling their feathers and taking me under their wing. Before I knew what was happening, I was seated on the sofa by their desk with a plastic cup of water in my hand and a plate of biscuits on the coffee table in front of me. The girls hustled back to the desk and launched a very intense, hushed conversation about what must have been very important business. I recognised two of the girls from the Christmas party, but the third one was new. I could tell she was feeling it as well. She was constantly fluttering around the other two girls; she laughed just a second too late or raised her voice just a touch too loud when they were whispering. She received side glances that constantly cut her short and reminded her that she was new and shouldn't step out of line. She was probably temping.

"I'm just going to pop to the loo," I mouthed, pointing at the guest toilets by the entrance.

"Okay," they mouthed back. I had to cross the entrance to reach the toilets, and I almost went straight through it. There was nothing stopping me from walking out that door right there and then without looking back. The only reason I stayed was because I could imagine the look on Fiona's face if I told her I bolted.

I'm here now. I may as well see it through to the watery grave.

I headed to the same stall I camped out in on the morning of my interview. I remember reaching into my pocket for my list of potential questions I might be asked and not being able to read them because I was shaking so much. I didn't actually pee that morning either. I just sat in the cubicle, breathing.

Deep breaths, Barbara. You've got this.

I looked at my watch. I had two minutes until I was due to meet Dan. I took one last breath, and the stench of bleach hit the back of my throat.

Time to go Barbara.

Coughing, I unlocked the cubicle door, smoothed my skirt down and went back to sea.

Dan was sitting in my seat; a pile of biscuit crumbs sat on my plate and my plastic cup was empty. He smiled up at me.

"I don't like things to go to waste." Crumbs flew out of his mouth, and we both laughed. I instantly relaxed. "It's good to see you, Barbara."

He stood up, smiling at me, chewing his way through the last of a custard cream biscuit.

"Shall we?" He gestured past the girls and into the main office space.

I took his invite and headed past the rocks. I could feel the Sirens' eyes on my back burning a hole through my jacket. The office looked busy. Everyone looked like they had something to do or somewhere to be. Anyone would have thought we were preparing to go underground for the winter. Oops, look at that, Aiden. I said we.

"Where am I going, Dan?"

We walked past my desk. It was empty—completely empty. Normally, whenever we had an empty desk in the office, someone moved in the next day to either get away from Steve with the flaky skin condition or the corner that gets no natural light. Or, the desk gets used to store the bits that no one can quite bring themselves to get rid of. Yet there was my old desk, completely empty.

"We'll go to my office. It's moved now, by the way. I'm next to the kitchen. There's a certain few that I need to keep an eye on. I'll give you two guesses."

"Barbrini!" Rachel bounded out of the kitchen, spilling tea all over her hand. "Shit...that's hot. Damn it. BARB! How *are* you?"

Speak of the devil, and she shall appear.

"Hey, Rach. You still here?" I smiled at her. It felt so good to see a familiar face.

"He couldn't get rid of me if he tried." Rachel winked and punched Dan on the arm. She spilt tea over his suit, and he rolled his eyes. Rachel, completely oblivious, snorted with laughter at her own joke.

"You coming back to join the slaughterhouse then, Barb? We've missed you around here."

"I...umm..." I didn't know.

"How long have you been on break now, Rachel?" Dan asked curtly. Rachel's cackle quickly subsided to a wobbly smile.

"I'll catch you later, Barbara." She spun on her heels, and her curly brown hair bobbed away between the cubicles. Little drops of tea trailed behind.

Dan sighed, pushed his new office door open and waved me inside. He'd had the walls replaced with glass, so he had an overview of the entire office. He also had a clear view of the kitchen, which I'm guessing was the most important part.

"It was either this or the kitchen had to go," he said, taking a seat across from me. He paused before speaking again. "Barbara."

"Daniel," I nodded back.

"It really is good to see you. You look healthy."

It's amazing what Fi can do with a touch of makeup. Thank

you, Fi.

"Thanks, Dan." I looked around the office. "How's it been?"

"Honestly or professionally?"

"Honestly."

"It's been hell." He sighed and looked at his hands crossed on his desk. "I don't even know where to start."

I stayed silent.

"Your leaving really took a toll on us. I don't mean anything against you by that, of course. But with everything that happened to you, we had a lot of staff re-evaluating their lives. I had countless one-on-ones with people who were suddenly unhappy with their current position. I'm not only talking about within the company, but in their lives. I was in way over my head. We had quite a few fantastic employees leave after you, and no one in the office has been the same since."

I kept my mouth shut. I couldn't trust myself to speak, and I wanted to see where he was going with the discussion. He leaned back in his chair and began chewing the skin around his nails.

"No one has gone near your desk since you left. No one. It's like a shrine. Rachel wipes it down every now and again, and she actually hissed at me once when I tried to approach her while she was tending to it. She *hissed* at me, Barbara."

My insides swelled with pride at Rachel's loyalty.

"The truth is, Barbara, we really need you back. I completely understand if you don't want to or aren't ready to. But, if you are, it would do wonders for the morale of the team around here. Perhaps you could even go part time? We all miss you, Barb." He made eye contact with me, before glancing over my shoulder.

He continued. "I'm sorry to throw this all on you so quickly. I didn't plan for the conversation to go like this. Hell, I didn't plan this conversation at all. I'm sorry. What do you think?"

The truth is, Aiden, the conversation couldn't have gone any better. It was exactly what I needed and wanted.

Dan was off again. "Of course, you don't even need to come back to your old role if you don't want to. I'm sure I could find something else for you. We'll give you as much or as little as you like. I mean, if you come back. It's entirely your decision. Come back?"

I'd never seen Dan like that. He was utterly helpless. If I'd seen this Dan a few years ago, I probably would have laughed in his face. But in that moment, I admired his honesty. I also remembered what Fi told me—I shouldn't agree to anything today. Yet, I felt obliged not to play games with him.

"Dan, I will come back. I want to."

His hands dropped into his lap and his shoulders slumped an inch.

"I just want to speak with my sister about what we think is good for me. But know that I want to come back, and the sooner the better." I smiled at him.

"Thank God for that."

While you're at it, could you ask him when he's giving my son back?

I stood up and Dan followed suit. He offered his hand to me across the desk.

"Oh, fuck it." He came around the desk and hugged me. I felt his hard chest against mine and noticed his heart was beating just a touch faster than it should. I hugged him back with my hands low on his back. His arms felt good around me, and he smelt fantastic. He stepped away. "I can't wait to have you back,

Barbara."

My face grew red hot. "Thanks Dan, I'll give you a ring in a couple of days, okay?"

"Please do."

I turned on my heels, my face growing hotter by the second. I wanted to get my jacket off; sweat was suddenly pouring from my armpits. I threw open his office door and walked straight into Rachel, knocking a cold cup of tea over both of us.

"Oh, shit. Sorry, Rach. I didn't even see you..."

"You're coming back!" she squealed. I scoffed a laugh.

"Rachel! That meeting was confidential," I said.

"It's Dan's fault for moving his office next to the kitchen, the walls are thin."

"They are, indeed, Rachel." Dan shouted from his office. "Go make yourself useful!"

We laughed, and Rachel grabbed my hand, leading me to her desk.

"You are going to come back, right? That wasn't just you being polite, was it? We need you back here."

"I just have to figure out what I want to do, and then I'll join you guys again."

"Rachel!" Dan's head was poking out of his office door. "If I have to say your name one more time today, the kitchen goes."

She spun back to me like we were caught in a war zone.

"Shit, okay. Go, go. I'll hide a bottle of Cava in the second fridge for your return." She winked at me and snorted with laughter.

I missed that girl. I squeezed her arm and took off, leaving her alone on the battlefield. I breezed past the Sirens on my way out.

"See you soon, girls," I called.

"Bye, Barbara," they sung. I didn't look at them. I kept my head high. This place needed me. I had purpose again.

I got home in record-breaking time. I couldn't wait to tell Fi what happened. The whole thing couldn't have gone better if we'd tried. I let myself in.

"Hello? Fi? Boys?"

"We're up here, Aunty Barbara." Fred's head poked over the top of the stairs. Jack's was quick to follow.

"You've got a visitor," said Jack.

"Mummy says we're to stay out of sight," whispered Fred. I looked at the kitchen door. I don't think I'd seen it closed since I moved into this place. It looked odd. Had it always been white?

I pushed open the door. Fi was sitting at my kitchen table. Oliver was sitting opposite her. My mouth went dry. The swelling had gone down around his eye. He had a fresh-looking patch stuck to his eye, and his eyebrow had begun growing back.

"Don't tell me you bought a dishwasher because of me," she said.

I closed the kitchen door and stayed with my back to it. My face grew hot for the second time today.

"He told me everything, Barbara." She stood up, shaking her head with her face in her hands. Oliver fidgeted in his seat, not meeting my stare.

"Did you lose your eye?" I asked. He shook his head.

"You should go, Oliver. Thank you for being so honest with me," Fi said.

He mumbled something under his breath before getting out of his chair. He kept his head down and slipped out the back door.

"And here I was thinking you were better, Barb? What on

Earth were you thinking? You know what? Don't answer that. I don't want to know." She kept shaking her head at me and suddenly all the air that Dan had filled me with let itself out.

"I am better though, Fi. I promise you I'm better. Having you and the boys here has been so good for me."

"We both know this is temporary, Barb. I thought you were better before I arrived. I thought you got your life back on track."

Is that what you did to me, Aiden? You knocked me off track?

"But hell, you bought a damn dishwasher because Oliver's mother sliced your face open! After you nearly blinded her son!" Her voice grew louder with every word.

"Dan asked me to come back to the office."

"Well, that's bloody brilliant, Barbara. I'm sure he'll be thrilled to know he's hiring a woman that should be in jail for grievous bodily harm—of a FUCKING CHILD! Which, by the way, still might happen. That family doesn't owe you anything, Barbara, not one morsel of forgiveness. You want to know why we ended up talking today? He saw my boys playing in the front garden and he told them you were a bad person. He wanted to *warn* them about you. Can you imagine how confused I was when they called me outside?"

There was a clatter from the hallway behind me. Fi stormed across the kitchen and threw the door open. Fred and Jack tumbled in.

"Upstairs, NOW!" she roared, and the boys scurried away with their tails between their legs. She spun back to me.

"You cannot be done for assault, Barbara. Your life, our lives, would be over. Mother must be turning in her grave." She threw her hands in the air. "You know it won't even just be assault. You could be done for grooming as well. You'll be known as a child groomer. You'll be branded a paedophile, Barbara. Do you know what that sort of thing does to someone? Do you know what it could do to their entire family?"

I burst into tears.

Why is she shouting at me, Aiden? I was only trying to make things right for us.

"You are going 'round to their place, and you will do whatever that woman wants from you to convince her not to press charges," she hissed.

"I can't go back there."

"I don't care what you think you can or can't do, Barbara. You don't have a choice anymore. Your shitty decisions are no longer just affecting you. You're hurting people, Barbara. You're physically hurting people. I don't even want my kids to be around you anymore."

"Fi, I would never!"

"Really, Barbara? What makes you so sure about that?" She stormed into the hall. "Boys, grab your things we're leaving!"

"What!?" Fred whined from the top of the stairs.

"Do not even think about giving me lip right now. Pack your things, we are going." Her eyes were on fire. The boys knew they were out of their depth and began running around the house throwing everything they could into their overnight bags. Fi turned back to me, lowering her voice now that the boys were within earshot.

"If she presses charges, this is all going to court. If this goes to court, you know it's going to be all over the papers. Your name, OUR name. I can't bring my sons up with their friends thinking they've got a paedophile for an aunt." She shook her head at Fred, who was handling a packet of week-old Pick 'n Mix that had melted together. "Bin it."

"But, it's still good!" he argued.

"Fred!" He was silenced with dragon eyes again. I watched him run into the front room before turning back to my sister.

"Please stop using that word," I begged.

"Which one? Paedophile? If you don't like it, I can think of a few others. I'm sure our neighbours can think of a thousand more, too. Let's see: pervert, psychopath, child molester."

"Fi, stop." Tears streamed down my face. My sister was always on my side. She defended me through everything, yet here she was spewing hate at me after all of our years together.

"Boys! I don't care if you're packed or not. If you're not by the front door in exactly 30 seconds, there will be no pocket money for a month." One of the boys screamed. I couldn't tell which one.

"Here's what is going to happen. You're going to go 'round to that boy's house and apologise profusely to his mother. You are going to get on your knees and beg for it if you need to. You're going to pray to every God there is that she doesn't press charges because if she does, I won't be here to pick up the pieces. Not this time, Barbara. I have a family of my own to think of."

I nodded and cried, snot poured from my nose.

"I love you, Barbara. I just have no fucking clue who you are anymore."

She stormed to the front door and flung it open.

"Mummy said a bad word," Fred mumbled, his sleeping bag trailing out of his rucksack.

The front door slammed shut, and I was left in silence. I fell to my knees. The dishwasher pinged, signalling that it had finished its cycle.

The letterbox opened. "Bye, Aunty Barbara!"

I got up and left the house. I didn't bother with shoes. I wandered aimlessly around the streets. I was ushered from place to place as I made various art galleries and shop fronts look tacky. My eyes finally fell upon *Rainbow Avenue*, the paint store, in which, all that time ago, I invested in 13 cans of *Daffodil White* to drown out the *Baby Blue* of our not so baby, but very blue, future together. Your nursery had been my Everest.

I floated into the store, and the aisles blurred past me like I had been swallowed by a cartoon. I drifted down its throat and eased into its bowels. I stopped as my eyes locked on what I'd been looking for. A can to the right of *Laura Ashley's Faded Gold* and just under *Crown's Golden Cream* was simply, in all its beauty, *Gold*. It didn't say who it was by. It was probably made by the Gods. Probably made especially for a Ms. Barbara Bridges. I snatched up the can before other shoppers followed my line of sight and swooped in, green as Envy, to try to pinch our gold from us. One can is enough. One can will be all we need to start over.

I arrived back home and cracked open the lid before I was even through the front door. I allowed the sweet golden fumes to fill my nostrils, flood my lungs, and lift my head that little bit higher. My chin was up. I thought of Oliver and the pain I caused him. I took the rippling tin over to the work surface and placed it out of harm's way. I ran upstairs and grabbed your bottle from the chest of drawers. I filled your bottle and put it in the microwave.

I popped a jelly cube into my mouth. The ping of the microwave broke my gaze on the tin of liquid gold. I grabbed your bottle and the paint tin and floated upstairs. I felt like I managed to capture the lighter tones of Dr. Demigod's hair, snip off the linings of your clouds, shave the little stars from your rattle, melt them all down and stir them into our remedy for this *oopsy daisy*. The sign on your bedroom door greeted me.

Aiden's Room

Looking down at our remedy gave me strength. This would be a new start for us. We didn't need Fi. We didn't need the Harps. It must be you and me, as it always has been and as it always should be.

Specks and splashes of *Daffodil White* scarcely covered your *Baby Blue*. My feet sunk into the carpet as I took in your crib and your favourite teddy bear that I tore to pieces. The teddy bear's only remaining eye still mocked me. I tore the eye free from its socket and plopped it into our cure. I watched it first float, sending mini tidal waves around the tin, before it became engulfed. It tipped like the *Titanic* and plunged to the murky golden depths of our Atlantic Ocean. Your baby shower gifts were a splash of colour against the white and blue speckled walls. I walked around the room running my hands along your walls. Little puffs of talc plumed out from the carpet underfoot.

I set the paint tin down, completely mesmerised by the way it shimmered. It caught the fragmented light from the costume crystals of your dream catcher in the window. I dipped my free hand into the paint and watched it disappear briefly before re-emerging a glorious gold. It was coated in beauty fit for Athena. I held my hand to the wall and nodded in approval as more fumes soaked through my senses. My head floated, skimming the ceiling as I let the first few drops of paint from my fingertips drop onto my outstretched toes. The first touch was cold, and I almost withdrew. But the beauty of it, Aiden. I was transforming in our room, eternal, captured in time under sheets of gold.

The paint trickled down my arms as I took swig after swig from your bottle. Your drink burnt my throat. Did I leave it in the microwave too long?

My body began to cool the liquid. It embraced our remedy. Your rattle started to play, quietly at first, filling the air around me like distant church bells. The more we painted though, the louder it got, and I wanted it to never stop. With both my hands, I painted our walls—wave after wave of glorious gold. The paint dripped down my arms. *I want to be Mumsy.* I raised my hands to my face and let gold run from my head and down my neck. I wanted it to encase me. I want to stay eternal for you. I finished your bottle and let your bedtime drink seep through my system. The thick smell of gold was overwhelming, but I am a God now. I can handle this and so can you. My fingernails scraped the bottom of the paint tin. I admired our artwork.

My gaze drifted around *Baby Blues* merging with *Daffodil Whites* and all of it was lined with a glorious, shimmering gold. It was enlightening, Aiden. I moved over to your drawers and found the talcum powder once more. I opened it and sent white plumes above my head. I outstretched my golden arms as I fell through our clouds and on to our crib. My eyes traced the last few trickles of gold as they wound paths down the interior of your bottle. Gold runs with my blood. Your music was calling so loud, so beautiful. I took a great lungful of heavenly air as my eyes contently rested. I recalled your figure, your tiny little feet with tiny little toes. That frame I was so worried I wouldn't fall instantly in love with.

Aiden? I gasped, inhaling all I could of your golden heart, as it pumped in time with mine. It lifted me higher...

Aiden? Your music. Your music is glorious. Your golden tones resound through me. They are so strong.

Aiden, My Love? I can hear you. I can feel your tiny little hands around mine. I won't let you go this time, My Love. I've got you now. Do you hear me, too?

Golden tears cut paths down my face. They cut paths that find your feet and lead you to me. I was right. You are walking, and you are marvellous at it.

The crystals from your dream catcher shatter at the window and rain down upon us as we fall asleep among a thousand dreams and, together, dream of a thousand nights.

"I hear you, Mum. Let's rest now...

About the Author

Ray Slater Berry was born and raised in London, United Kingdom. Writing poetry and short stories from a young age, Ray went on to study English Literature and Creative Writing at Falmouth University. After earning his undergraduate degree, he completed an MA in Professional Writing, where *Golden Boy* was first started.

After University, Ray moved back to London where he worked for a social media marketing agency. Not happy with his balance between life and work, Ray relocated to Barcelona. In Barcelona, Ray continued to write while working as Head of Creative Strategy for a global travel and education company. He also competed in beach volleyball tournaments up and down the Spanish coastline.

Ray took the summer of 2017 to pursue his writing career full-time and to finish writing *Golden Boy*. Ray is currently working on his second novel, *Kelly and the Willow Tree*.

26216633R00161

Printed in Great Britain
by Amazon